Praise for *I Choose Peace*

"I Am Second provides an honest look at how others have found peace in their lives through a relationship with Christ. The stories each person shares reflect real life struggles we can all relate to and how each found their encouragement in Christ."

—**JOE GIBBS,** Pro Football Hall of Fame coach, NASCAR Hall of Fame owner

"*I Choose Peace* reminds me that peace only comes from the Peace Maker and that always to be thankful and loving to my neighbors is the path to peace."

—**MICHAEL TAIT,** Newsboys lead singer

"I have been a fan of I Am Second since its founding more than ten years ago. I have seen the impact of its films and have been honored to sit in the white chair and declare myself 'second.' Everything I Am Second does is for one goal—to inspire people to put Jesus first. *I Choose Peace* does just that, and I can't recommend it enough."

—**ANNIE LOBERT,** founder of Hookers For Jesus and Destiny House

"For the past ten years, I Am Second has used powerful storytelling through film to show individuals from all walks of life putting Jesus first. In the same vein, I Am Second's newest book, *I Choose Peace*, has the opportunity to further inspire and help readers discover the true secret to fulfillment and wholeness is found in God."

—**STEVE GREEN,** president of Hobby Lobby Stores, Inc.; founder and chairman of the board of Museum of the Bible

I CHOOSE PEACE

I CHOOSE
PEACE

RAW STORIES OF REAL PEOPLE FINDING
CONTENTMENT AND HAPPINESS

Doug Bender

NELSON BOOKS
An Imprint of Thomas Nelson

© 2019 e3 Partners Ministry

All rights reserved. No portion of this book may be reproduced, stored in a retrieval system, or transmitted in any form or by any means—electronic, mechanical, photocopy, recording, scanning, or other—except for brief quotations in critical reviews or articles, without the prior written permission of the publisher.

Published in Nashville, Tennessee, by Nelson Books, an imprint of Thomas Nelson. Nelson Books and Thomas Nelson are registered trademarks of HarperCollins Christian Publishing, Inc.

Published in association with the literary agency of Wolgemuth & Associates, Inc.

Thomas Nelson titles may be purchased in bulk for educational, business, fund-raising, or sales promotional use. For information, please e-mail SpecialMarkets@ThomasNelson.com.

Any Internet addresses, phone numbers, or company or product information printed in this book are offered as a resource and are not intended in any way to be or to imply an endorsement by Thomas Nelson, nor does Thomas Nelson vouch for the existence, content, or services of these sites, phone numbers, companies, or products beyond the life of this book.

Unless otherwise noted, Scripture quotations are taken from the Holy Bible, New International Version®, NIV®. Copyright © 1973, 1978, 1984, 2011 by Biblica, Inc.™ Used by permission of Zondervan. All rights reserved worldwide. www.zondervan.com. The "NIV" and "New International Version" are trademarks registered in the United States Patent and Trademark Office by Biblica, Inc.™

ISBN 978-1-4002-1037-4 (eBook)
ISBN 978-1-4002-1694-9 (IE)

Library of Congress Cataloging-in-Publication Data

Names: Bender, Doug, author.
Title: I choose peace : raw stories of real people finding contentment and happiness / Doug Bender.
Description: Nashville : Thomas Nelson, 2019.
Identifiers: LCCN 2019006644 (print) | ISBN 9781400210367 (hardcover)
Subjects: LCSH: Christian biography. | Christian life.
Classification: LCC BR1700.3 .B463 2019 (print) | LCC BR1700.3 (ebook) | DDC 277.3/0830922 [B]--dc23
LC record available at https://lccn.loc.gov/2019006644
LC ebook record available at https://lccn.loc.gov/2019980229

Printed in the United States of America
19 20 21 22 23 LSC 10 9 8 7 6 5 4 3 2 1

To the Seconds
Whose Stories Remain
Though We See Them No More
Rod Bayron
Ethan Hallmark
Ken Hutcherson
David McKenna
Nathan Schroer

Contents

Introduction xi

Finding Peace in **Love** and **Loss**

1. *Bliss:* my love and my loss 5
   Kathie Lee Gifford, TV personality
2. *Opposites:* the surprise of love 17
   Chip and Joanna Gaines, former hosts of HGTV's *Fixer Upper*
3. *Friend:* for the lonely soul 27
   Lee Yih, businessman
4. *Family:* sometimes it takes a fight 39
   Phil and Kay Robertson, stars of A&E's *Duck Dynasty*

Finding Peace in **Identity** and **Purpose**

5. *Control:* why I gave it up 61
   Ben King, professional cyclist
6. *Thinker:* when God speaks through a fish 71
   Eric Metaxas, author and speaker

CONTENTS

7. *Perfect*: the beauty of failure Shawn Johnson, Olympic gymnast	85
8. *Happy*: the bigger game Albert Pujols, Major League Baseball all-star	99

9. *Shame*: I felt less than human
    R. A. Dickey, Major League Baseball pitcher and
    Cy Young Award winner
	111

10. *Race*: why I matter Jason "Propaganda" Petty, hip-hop artist, activist	129

Finding Peace in **Difficulty** and **Disappointment**

11. *Trapped*: when Jesus makes it worse Brian "Head" Welch, Korn lead guitarist	143
12. *Beauty*: I was ugly and ruined Lauren Scruggs Kennedy, lifestyle blogger	159
13. *Pain*: the thief came Austin Carlile, former lead vocalist for Of Mice & Men	169
14. *Expectations*: in-n-out of failure Lynsi Snyder, owner of In-N-Out Burger	183
15. *Worry*: tapping out of the fight Cody Garbrandt, mixed-martial-arts champion	195
16. *Peace*: when we lost Hope Doug Bender, author	207

Acknowledgments	219
Notes	221
About the Author	223

Introduction

Peace.

It's what we are all looking for.

We look for it in relationships. We search for it in our jobs or in dropping that last five pounds. We try to win it, earn it, or buy it, propelled by that intangible, all-powerful urge at the base of our souls.

We may not call it peace. We may say we're searching for happiness, contentment, purpose. But we definitely know when we don't have it.

Our lack of peace shows in our overstuffed closets full of clothes we never wear. It reveals itself in our complaints about work and our fights at home. It glares in our vain search for more affirmation, more accolades, more likes—and in the anxiety that stalks so many of us.

According to the National Institute of Mental Health, one in five of us experiences an anxiety disorder in a given year and one in three experiences one at some point in our lives.[1] Most

INTRODUCTION

go undiagnosed. Often we don't know the name of that itch in our souls. We just know something is wrong. We feel lonely even when surrounded by people. We work too hard and play too frantically. We self-medicate and overindulge. We keep on asking life why? Why us? What now?

These are all attempts at finding peace. None of us would care who we were, what we had, or who we had if we had an underlying sense of peace.

Peace tells our hearts that everything's okay. It speaks to the mind and removes the worry and the doubt. It calms the emotions and soothes the spirit. No matter what life has for us, when we have peace we can smile and feel secure.

Are you happy with your work? Do your relationships bring you joy? Do you know who you are and why you're here? If not, you'll find yourself filling life with noise so you can't hear the emptiness.

But your life can have a different story. It's a story that so many have experienced through the I Am Second movement. I Am Second began as a website with a handful of films. It has since spread the message of peace to millions by telling the raw, beautiful, broken human stories of people just like you.

That's exactly the kind of stories you'll find in this book. They are the stories of people who looked for peace but couldn't find it. They tried drugs, work, love, and everything in between, but they never found peace in these. They didn't find peace in a bottle or in a pill. They didn't find it when they fell in love or got that job. They looked in all the places you have looked, but they found it only in Jesus. For many, Jesus was the last place they ever

INTRODUCTION

cared to look, a place they'd sworn never to look. But finally they did, and there it was.

Peace doesn't get you out of the pain. It gets you through it.

It doesn't remove you from the craziness. It removes the craziness from you.

It doesn't take away the nasty comments, the frowny-face emojis, or the dirty look someone gave you. It just says, "I've got you."

Peace is you smiling at the thunder and laughing at the wind, not because you control the storm, but because you know that the One who does is on your side. That's the peace the people in this book found. That's the peace they chose when they chose Jesus.

Finding Peace in Love and Loss

Love offers the greatest highs and the deepest lows.
Nothing compares to falling in love, and nothing despairs like falling out of it. Love holds both the beauty of God and the frailty of humanity. But whether we encounter it in friendship, family, or romance, human love reveals only a foggy glimpse of the more perfect thing. It whets our appetite for something more. Love here on earth never lives up to the hype, but it does give us a taste of something better to come.

If you've ever wished for more love in your life or more from the love you have, these stories are for you. They are the stories of people who found peace in love and loss. They are the lonely souls and the broken hearts. They sought companionship, passion, and family. Some found it. Some had it and lost it. But all of them discovered a greater love in the process, a love that gave them peace.

Chapter 1
Bliss

my love and my loss

KATHIE LEE GIFFORD, TV PERSONALITY

Wouldn't it be a wonderful feeling," asks Kathie Lee Gifford, former cohost of NBC's fourth hour of the *Today* show, "to wake up in the morning and understand that no matter what goes on today, God can make something good out of it?"

Kathie Lee says she was born to entertain. If you were to meet her, you would be tempted at first to think you were encountering someone doing a slapstick version of herself. But it's just Kathie Lee being Kathie Lee. She didn't get in front of a camera and discover her television personality; instead, the performer came first and the camera followed.

Kathie Lee's father told her many times while she was growing up to "find something you love to do and then figure out a way to get paid for it." Kathie Lee did exactly that. She always knew God made her to perform, and she knew the entertainment industry was where she would fulfill her destiny. In fact, she earned her first paycheck as an entertainer when she was just ten years old.

"It was thrilling getting my first paying job singing," she says. "I knew exactly what I wanted to do from the time I was a baby. But to be a young woman in that business is brutal because of the rejection. It's nonstop."

After a dozen years working as a singer and actress, Kathie Lee rose to national fame cohosting a live morning television show with Regis Philbin in 1985. Beginning locally in New York, *Live with Regis and Kathie Lee* sprang to national syndication three years after she joined the program and became an American mainstay. Until the summer of 2000, she cohosted the show, which aired on millions of television sets every weekday morning.

She was in her element, doing what she had been born to do, what her parents had always encouraged her to do. But Kathie Lee's mom and dad had never pushed her to perform.

"I've never understood the kind of parent that says to their children, 'You've got to be this or that,'" Kathie Lee says. "I was privileged to have parents like I had. They were extraordinary, loving people. They loved me for who I was and encouraged my dreams."

Growing up, she always had a song to sing and a show to perform. She found fulfillment in bringing joy and a smile to others. Her always-on-stage approach to life followed her throughout the years.

"I learned the reason that performing was so joyful to me is because God is our creator," she says. "I am created by God, and I'm made in his image. That means I am also a creator. I feel most divine when I am creating something beautiful. It's every human being's purpose."

Kathie Lee's joy is not a result of a lucky career or perfect family, as is clear when she speaks of the darker points in her journey. She may have earned eleven Daytime Emmy nominations, written books, released albums, and even contributed to several Broadway productions. But the brighter the limelight shines, the more caustic public reactions to a stumble can turn.

In 1996, reports surfaced that Kathie Lee's clothing line was produced out of a Honduran sweatshop with abysmally poor working conditions. The reports held her personally responsible. She insisted she had nothing to do with the day-to-day operating of the clothing factories and was only a celebrity sponsor of the apparel. She even worked to bring about legislation to prevent similarly inhumane working conditions elsewhere. But still the public reaction came fierce and hard.

"It was a very dark, dark period for me," she says. "But God put me to work. There is slavery in the world, more than ever. There are labor conditions that are horrible."

"It's unjust what you've been accused of," she heard God say through all this, "but why don't you get your eyes off of you for a minute and look at the unjust conditions that people are working under. You didn't cause it, but you need to care about it."

She became a leading proponent of fair labor laws and used her on-air power to push for legislative changes.

In the following year, Kathie Lee's personal life also hit a new low. Kathie Lee had married Frank Gifford in 1986, and after more than a decade of marriage and two children, Frank was caught in a humiliating and public affair. Tabloids seized upon the story and printed pictures that brought agony to Kathie Lee.

"It was devastating to me," she says. "But I was able to stay in my marriage and have God heal it. I've heard from hundreds of thousands of people since then who got courage from [my experience], courage to stay in their broken marriages and forgive their husbands and wives. They got courage to keep their families together. Not everybody does. I didn't do it on my own. God gives us everything we need every day."

Kathie Lee's journey with God began as a child when Jesus called her name in a dream.

"It's vivid to me to this day," she recalls. "In the dream I'm outside in the front yard helping my daddy rake the leaves. We used to play in them. I looked up. There was Jesus sitting on a cloud. He smiled at me and he said my name."

A few years later, as a twelve-year-old, she walked into a movie theater featuring *The Restless Ones*, a production of the Billy Graham Evangelistic Association. The movie has been widely panned for its stiff dialogue and overt religiosity, but for many the truth at its core outshone any artistic inadequacies. It told of a young girl on the cusp of womanhood making the choice between going down the road that led to death or one that led to life.

"I could hear the voice of the Lord in the movie," Kathie Lee says.

"Kathie," she heard him say, "will you trust me to make something beautiful out of your life and go down my road? It's harder. It's going to be lonely at times. It's going to be tougher than the big wide road over there. Ultimately it's going to be a much more beautiful life, but you've got to trust me."

After the movie, as with all Billy Graham events, someone rose in the front and asked if anyone wanted to come forward and follow Jesus. The movie, cheesy as it was, served a function for the more than 120,000 people who'd said yes to that question during the time it ran. Kathie Lee was in that number.

"I've made a lot of mistakes in my life since then," she says. "I will make a lot of them before this day is done. But that is one decision I made that I have always been deeply, deeply grateful for. I listened to the voice of Jesus. I heard him tell me he had a purpose for my life, that he loved me. He wanted to make something beautiful with my life."

Kathie Lee has Jewish ancestry, and as a Christian she has discovered great significance in a Hebrew word that is found in Jewish greetings, teachings, and scriptures: *shalom*. The word touches upon the idea of perfection and wholeness.

"*Shalom* doesn't mean just peace," she says, "like it's come to mean in our world. It means all of the aspects of God. It means justice, righteousness, faithfulness, unfailing love, and, yes, peace. It's a peace that passes all understanding. That's what we're here for. Look around. Do you see the chaos? You're supposed to be part of the shalom, the peace. That's what every human heart longs for—to partner in that and know you matter."

The Bible calls Jesus the Prince of Peace. He's the one who

brings peace and wholeness to the world. But he didn't sit on that peace and hoard it for himself. He stepped out of heaven and got dirty with his people. He lived with them, ate with them, hugged them, and talked with them. He taught his followers to join him in this work of getting out and bringing peace to the world.

Kathie Lee finds inspiration in Jesus' example. Jesus got out into the world and confronted the cultural norms of his day. He insisted on spending time with the poor, the sick, the sinner, and the outcast.

For fifteen years on *Live with Regis and Kathie Lee*, Kathie Lee lived her life publicly, discussing family, marriage, and raising children on a morning talk show for the world to see. People saw her cry, laugh, and ask the deeper questions. After leaving *Live*, she took some time away from television, then rejoined America's morning routine in 2008 as cohost with Hoda Kotb of NBC's fourth hour of *Today*. For the next decade Kathie Lee continued to follow Jesus' example of getting out into the world.

"We are supposed to get out and be the sweet fragrance of Jesus to this world," she says. "Love your neighbor as you love yourself is what Jesus taught. Don't live in a selfie world. Live in a selfless world. Don't walk over homeless people on your way to get someplace. We're supposed to get down and dirty like Jesus did. We're supposed to wash AIDS patients' feet. We're supposed to adopt children who have no home.

"God is perfecting us. Not a physical perfection or personal perfection, but God's perfect love. He is perfecting love in us. That love leads to perfection in a world yet to come. It's something to look forward to."

Kathie Lee's husband, Frank Gifford, passed away in 2015 after more than fifty years in the public eye. Frank had been a star running back for the University of Southern California before embarking on a stellar twelve-year career with the New York Giants. He made eight Pro Bowl appearances and won the league's Most Valuable Player award. He then turned to broadcasting and went on to host twenty-seven years of *Monday Night Football*. An entire generation knew Frank Gifford as the play-by-play announcer for football's greatest games. But the expression Kathie Lee found on his face when he died said more to her than anything he had ever said on air. His eyes looked upward, as to heaven, a look of amazement frozen on his face.

"From that moment on I had the peace that passes all understanding," she says. "He saw Jesus, and Jesus took his breath away. I was so happy for him. Frank is exactly where he's supposed to be now. So is my mother; so is my father. I have so many friends who have passed on through the years. I don't want life to be all about what I've lost.

"That's the dilemma for people as they age. People start dying all around them, and there's a hopelessness that can creep in. I don't want to live my life in hopelessness. I've been there. But I've found a joy that has nothing to do with circumstances. That's a hard place to find. But it's a worthy journey and a worthy search."

Through the many trials and joys of a career in the limelight and a private life made public, Kathie Lee has learned the secret to peace and joy. It's not something that your environment dictates or that luck can steal. It's based on something more sure and lasting.

"My joy is nonnegotiable," she says, quoting her personal mantra. "That's the beginning of bliss in your life—when you understand where your joy comes from and you protect it with everything in you. I've always known where my joy came from."

Kathie Lee has learned through experience that popularity and friendship come and go. Even a spouse can betray you or leave you. But she's also learned that relationships here on earth open up a window into the greater beyond and a greater relationship.

"You have to let [God] touch you," she says. "You have to get up out of your seat, like I did, and walk toward him. You have to trust like I did so many years ago in that darkened little movie theater. He's going to do what he says. He's going to love you. If you're broken, he's going to love you back to life. If you're sick, he's going to heal you. It may not be the way you think, but he's going to heal that place in your life that is not right. He's going to help you forget the things that haunt you. He's not only going to be your comforter. He'll be your pillow, too, the one that you cry into. He loves you with an everlasting love."

Kathie Lee Gifford discovered a deep and lasting peace through Jesus. It's not peace that looks traditionally churchy or religious. It's raw and authentic. She laughs with God, and she cries with him. She has found a rock on which to rely when the tragic or the unexpected comes.

That peace showed up after someone invited her down the aisle at a movie theater. It came through the countless interactions she had on air, and it showed up in the eyes of her husband as he passed. The peace came from God, but it flowed through the many people and relationships that God sent her way.

We don't always expect God to be working through the words and actions of others. We wish he would jump out of the clouds and speak to us directly. But God seems to enjoy doing just the opposite of what we expect.

Kathie Lee learned that.

And so did reality stars Chip and Joanna Gaines, whose story comes next.

Chapter 2
Opposites

the surprise of love

CHIP AND JOANNA GAINES, FORMER HOSTS OF HGTV'S *FIXER UPPER*

If you've ever watched HGTV's reality show *Fixer Upper*, you'll quickly be amazed by two things.

First, apparently you should be able to rehab a kitchen, paint several bedrooms, and retile a shower in a weekend.

Second, Chip and Joanna, the married stars of the show, are as different as two people can be.

Rather than let their differences wedge them apart, however, Chip and Joanna let love surprise them into discovering their full potential. Even in the way they describe each other, they find a way to both be themselves and inspire each other to be more.

"Chip is the riskiest person I've ever met," Joanna says. "I've yet to find anything that scares him. If you give Chip a boundary, he's going to break that boundary. If you give him a rule, he's not going to follow it. If you tell him you can't go past this line, he'll put his toe over it. The moment I think I've figured him out, he surprises me. If I didn't have Chip Gaines in my life, I'd still be dreaming in my head but not acting on any of my dreams. When we got together, I felt like I was really living life for the first time."

"Be yourself" is a saying you've likely seen or heard fifteen times already today. The idea behind the phrase takes on several different flavors. One is the "forget the world" variety, which tells us to throw out all social conventions, all care or thought of others and their opinions, and just do what we feel like. But then we realize this won't work because we actually do care about what other people think. And that's not a bad thing. In fact, it's a good thing to want and even need this kind of connection to others.

There is also the "you're perfect just the way you are" version of "be yourself," which insists that personal growth, life improvement, and wanting to be a better person betray your true self. Just be your own flawed self. Let the chips fall as they may. But a world where no one cares to grow or improve sounds like a new kind of hell. That's a world with no apologies and no forgiveness, no aha moments, and no newness. That's not a world any of us wants. We all have things to apologize for and new places to try to get to.

Maybe what we should mean by "be yourself" is that we each have a unique purpose in life. You can want to be loved by others and still be yourself. You can want to grow and still be yourself. Maybe being ourselves isn't a commitment to static individualism, but a commitment to our own unique journey to fullness. "Be yourself" can mean I'll be me, you be you, and together each of us can be more of who we were meant to be. That's the balance the Gaineses have found in their relationship.

"You're so unique to me," Chip says to Joanna. "You required so much effort to draw you out, because you had so little interest in being drawn out. You could just sit there and literally be content with that. The whole experience is still happening. Thirteen years later, and I still have as many questions about you as I do answers."

"Chip is such an open book," Joanna says in response. "There's nothing that he hasn't told the world. He makes fun of himself. He'll say what he thinks and do what he wants. There's no hiding. There's nothing that he wouldn't let me say or that he wouldn't want people to know. But I'm an internalizer, so things take longer for me to process. I'll know why I am having a bad day in two days, because I will have processed it. For Chip, I think it could get frustrating sometimes to not know what's in my head. But sometimes I really don't know!"

"Sometimes I think he forgets that we're different," Joanna says. "I need to have A through Z all lined up before I'm ready to make a decision. Chip is the very opposite. A through Z can line up later, but he's going to go ahead and take that step."

But it's not so much the speed of her husband's decisions that shocks Joanna as his willingness to risk failure, his entrepreneurial spirit. Certain people hope to get a job; people like Chip make their own job and thrive in the risk/reward lifestyle of running your own business. Years before HGTV launched the pilot episode of *Fixer Upper* in May 2013, Chip and Joanna ran their own business remodeling homes.

"I've always been an entrepreneur," Chip says. "When Jo and I met, I was flipping houses. I had two or three businesses other than the flipping business. Her dad would get me in the car and ask me how the job hunt was going. I never thought of getting a job. The worst argument we ever had related to this."

"I've never really been an insecure person," he says jokingly, adding, "I have almost inappropriately positive self-talk. When you think about the little voice in your ear that talks when you're being quiet, my little voice tells me how handsome I am. It tells me how funny I am, how rich I'm going to be. It's just constantly talking this positive feedback in my ear. Her dad is really the opposite of that. He would come over and start making assessments about the houses we lived in."

One night Chip had just finished a renovation on their current home and invited Joanna's parents over for dinner, hoping to impress them. While awaiting their arrival, Chip had a rare moment of self-doubt.

"I started looking around at the floor," he says. "I noticed some imperfections. I started realizing things I didn't do perfectly. I felt this overwhelming anxiety that her mom and dad were going to come into the house and rip it apart."

Chip, ever the open book, told Joanna of his anxieties. He complained of her parents' habit of judging his work and his professional choices. Joanna started defending her parents. And soon they were in the middle of the biggest fight they'd ever had. "Jo and I just went at it," Chip says.

Joanna happened to have a can of white primer paint in her hands as they shouted back and forth. She had been working on some last-minute touch ups. In a moment of anger, she slammed the can down on the table, forgetting that she had taken the lid off.

"This white primer came back and splashed her in her face," Chip remembers with a smile. "She literally just had this primer falling off of her eyelashes, falling off her nose, dripping off her chin and face. She looked like she'd been hit in the face with one of those whipped-cream pies. And she was just bawling her eyes out."

Obviously, Chip and Joanna made it past that particular fight. But as with many couples, their first year of marriage showed them that the very differences that fascinated them could also divide them.

"I was always struggling with this internal battle," she says, "going back and forth between wanting to be safe and wanting to change the world. I used to joke that my dream job was to sit at a desk. I'd have three file folders. At the end of the day, when I clocked out, the files would have been all put away. There's a part of me that's like that. I think to myself, 'If you do that thing, you could fail, so dream, but don't let it go any further than that.' That is where Chip comes in. Sometimes you do fail. But that's how we should live life."

Chip spent most episodes with a grin on his face, pushing for more and bigger. Joanna, always the sensible one, found a way to direct his boundless energy. Joanna the designer and Chip the lead contractor together found a way to turn the homeowners' dreams into reality each episode. His adventure and her order mixed to bring beauty to people's homes.

"Before Chip, my life was very safe," she says. "I would feel like God would want me to do something, and I'd always say no first. Then I'd question and I'd reason, and in two weeks I'd say, 'Okay, I'll do it.' God had a funny way of bringing me the reality of what it's like to follow Jesus. A lot of things are going to push you to a place of discomfort, to a place of freaking out."

Most people think peace in life means the lack of discomfort. They expect God to iron out all the wrinkles and smooth the rough spots. They even make decisions based on whether or not they feel peace about something. But that makes peace contingent on circumstance. That's a peace that only works when life goes smoothly. But life comes with bumps.

"I think if God is involved," Joanna says, "safe isn't necessarily the end goal. I feel like for the first time I'm really living life. My walk with God when I was little and all the way up until my twenties was always: if you play by the rules you'll be blessed. But then I met Chip. I feel like now it's when you take a step out in faith, that's where the greater reward is. God is really wanting us to take a further step. Faith used to be something that I did because I had to. Now I feel like faith is something I wouldn't want to live without. I don't want to be in the box any more. I don't want to play it safe."

Chip, too, has found his approach to faith changing because of his spouse's influence. "I have learned so much about order and structure through my wife," he says. "God is all of those things to me now. At the beginning, God was just chaotic to me. He was wild and unruly. I modeled my personality after that— the unbridled passion of God. Had I been born one hundred years prior, I would have been the guy on a horse riding off into the wilderness. Jo's idea of wild and crazy was staying up until ten o'clock with her parents watching a sitcom. When those two universes collided, somehow instead of fighting each other, those uniquenesses got us exploring each other's perspectives."

They both came to their relationship with a certain understanding of God and of themselves. They cast God in the image of their own strengths and dreams. But in coming together, they found a truer expression not only of God but of themselves as well. Chip's raw energy and adventurousness found its most positive expression through Joanna's stability. And Joanna found that her strength of character shone brightest when mixed with Chip's fearlessness.

"He's empowered me to do things I've been scared to do myself," Joanna says. "It's just peaceful. Even in this place we still have arguments, but it feels like we're pulling together and not pulling apart."

"My wife calmed a storm in me," Chip says. "I was a showman. I was crazy. I was trying to be so many people. But she calmed that storm in my heart and in my soul."

"As quirky and as embarrassing as it sounds, we really do complete each other," he says. "We really do have that weird way about each other where I feel more alive when I'm with her. We enjoy each other's company. We appreciate each other."

"She put me first in her life, just in the way that she admires me," he says. "I think I encourage her, and then she reciprocates by being enamored by that. It's sort of my nature to dote on people, to make people feel special. When I added that ingredient into her universe, she blossomed. She was like a flower in desperate need of water. I was water, and when the whole thing came together, she blossomed in a way that was really fascinating to watch. And in return I found stability, inspiration to be a better man, a better father and husband."

After five successful seasons of *Fixer Upper*, Chip and Joanna aired their final episode in April 2018. They have since announced they are in talks for their own lifestyle-focused media network. The details surrounding this opportunity remain a work in progress, but they hope to build a different kind of platform for unique, inspiring, and family-friendly content.

So-called reality television doesn't often come through on its promise of real-life authenticity. But Chip and Joanna's love story registers on the screen as utterly authentic. They have entertained us and taught us a lesson too. They've taught us the power of being the people God has designed us to be. That's what a relationship should do for two people. There is no more peaceful a place than authenticity. That doesn't mean there's not growth and potential that needs unlocking in each of us. But it does mean that we each are unique and wonderful, that we need to let who we are shine, and also that we can help it shine in someone else.

But not everyone has a relationship like Chip and Joanna's marriage. Some wander through life lonely, seeking a friend. If you've found loneliness to be your companion, then read on, because peace can be yours as well.

Chapter 3
Friend

for the lonely soul

LEE YIH, BUSINESSMAN

Loneliness visits us all at times. It's why we leave the television on in the background. It's the reason we can't drive without the radio on or ever set down the phone. The quiet lets the lonely cries of our heart ring out. Lee Yih heard those cries often while growing up.

"I was ashamed of being Chinese," Lee says. "In Mount Joy, Iowa, there were no other Chinese people apart from my family. I wanted so much to fit in."

His parents attended and met at nearby University of Iowa. Lee was born into a marriage of necessity, not love—and one that would end three years after it began.

"They married because she got pregnant," Lee says. "He wanted to go into the restaurant business. When that failed, he just took off."

Lee would grow up never knowing his biological father. And when his mother remarried years later, that marriage struggled as well.

"My mother blamed me for the difficulties. Behind closed doors my stepfather said, 'It's either him or me.' So I got shipped to Taiwan, ostensibly so I could learn Chinese."

Lee fought the move. He was fifteen and already struggling to make friends and fit in. Living in Taiwan, in a culture he neither knew nor appreciated, would only drive the loneliness deeper in his heart.

"I told my mother over and over that I hated being Chinese. I wanted to be white. I would not embrace my Chinese heritage. I was ashamed of being Chinese."

But Lee's mother, desperate to save her marriage, ignored her son's pleas. She had remarried when Lee was thirteen. Now he was out of the house at fifteen. He felt as displaced in Taiwan as he had in Iowa.

"I felt so Chinese in Iowa and so foreign in Taiwan," he says. Caught between two cultures, he had none to call his own. He had no template to forge his identity around. Estranged no matter where he lived or whom he surrounded himself with, he searched for answers, and he thought he would find them through material success. He dreamed of one day buying the love or appreciation he failed to inherit from family or culture.

"My dream has always been to be rich and successful," he says. "It was everything we didn't have. I grew up in a single-parent family before that was fashionable in America. We lived in a little apartment above a bar. I was so ashamed of that apartment.

I knew I wanted to be rich. That was my way to get respect, to get power, to get things that I wanted."

Lee returned to the US as a young man, studied finance, married, and set out to pursue the American dream, but his plans got derailed by the Vietnam draft. The army sent him to man a radar site in Germany, watching the Russians. He avoided Vietnam itself, but most of the guys in his unit had already done their tour and come back with the stories.

"They are talking about killing gooks," he says, referencing a racial slur commonly used of Vietnamese people. "I'm looking in the mirror and realize I'm a gook to these guys."

That was another painful blow, another reminder that Lee had never fit in. He was too Chinese to belong in Iowa, too American for Taiwan. His father abandoned him. His stepfather rejected him. His mother sent him away. And then he was surrounded by soldiers talking of killing people who looked similar to him.

"I was at the low point in my life in Germany," he says. "I'm in the army watching a radar screen for Russians who never came. I have no meaning to my life. I'm stoned all the time. Everybody is talking about killing gooks. And my marriage was also starting to fall apart."

Having never seen a marriage that worked, Lee struggled to know how to relate and function in such a relationship. At one point his wife, Miltinnie, told him she was going to leave him. It was just a matter of time.

"In my wife's thinking, I'm sure I was just a loser. I'm not functioning in life. I'm not functioning well in the army. I've got a big chip on my shoulder. So she tells me the marriage is over. I knew she meant it."

That's when they met a couple named June and David Otis. They became quick friends. The Otises invited them over to their house frequently. They were different. They reached out when no one else would. One night while over for dinner, Miltinnie asked them to explain.

"Why are you guys so different from other people?" she asked. Lee had wondered the same but was afraid to ask.

"We are different because we have a personal relationship with Jesus Christ," they answered.

"What does that mean?" Miltinnie asked.

It seemed a strange answer to Lee too. He had known about God since childhood, even attended a Lutheran parochial school, but he had heard nothing about a personal relationship with God. The emphasis at his school was on rules: live a good life, go to church, and watch your language. June and David introduced Lee to a new element, something unusual.

"I never dreamed that God could be my friend or that God could be my Father," Lee says. "Christianity was just a religion. It was at arm's length."

Lee had known the Otises were Christians, and he had known many Christians growing up. But the way June and David described their faith that evening shocked him and made him uncomfortable.

"I wanted to get out of there," Lee says. "But my wife got so interested in what they were saying. They started talking about Jesus as if he was a friend or a college buddy. It was like he was somebody living next door. She listened to what they said that night, and she started to change."

The change continued over the following weeks and months, as Miltinnie became more involved in learning about Jesus. For one thing, she stopped fighting with Lee. She seemed to look at him differently, with none of the contempt or annoyance. Other parts of her life started to change too. Eventually he followed her to gatherings at her new church. He expected to get what he always had: stares, rejection, politeness but no connection. But these people were different.

"These guys became my friends," he says. "I just felt the love of God. It was so strong. It just overwhelmed me. I could see it in everybody's eyes."

Lee didn't understand this kind of religion. This wasn't the God he'd grown up hearing about. This was someone who loved him and who somehow caused these people to love him too. He had no explanation, but the love hit him at his core. It felt unbelievable and irresistible. After one particular church gathering, he went home and talked to this God he wasn't sure even existed.

"If you're out there, and if you love me, I'd like to be included," he said.

This wasn't some glorious act of faith. It was feeble and simple. All he knew at that point was loneliness. If this God could change that, then he'd take all the love he could get. He didn't know if God wanted him, but if God was anything like this group of people, then maybe he would.

"I know exactly what it feels like to get picked last," he says, thinking of his childhood. "The last guy gets Lee, and then they argue about it. 'You take him.' 'No, you take him.' Nobody ever wanted me. I wanted so badly to fit in, to belong. And I never did"—until that moment in Germany when he asked God to be included.

"It's amazing what happened after I prayed this. I can't explain it. The world suddenly looked different from then on. I was a new creature. My life went straight up. It was weird."

Lee Yih left the army and went on to a successful financial career at Goldman Sachs, Morgan Stanley, and Lehman Brothers, achieving all the financial dreams he had held since his youth. He got the Mercedes and the big house. But those things never compared to what he found in Germany. There he had a community of people who loved him. He had a God who considered him a friend, someone with whom he now had a personal relationship.

"I call it a personal relationship because I talk to him," he says. "I love him, and he loves me. He knows and understands me. He's always with me. He's on my side. He's an advocate. He's rooting for me. Every time I've taken risks to follow him—every time—it's always worked out. I've been keeping track. I've got stories. He's never led me astray. He speaks to me through the Bible. It's uncanny the way he speaks personally."

After so many years of struggle, Lee found a place to belong—with God and his people. But having a personal relationship with God didn't instantly heal him of all his defects and insecurities. Money and career still pulled at his attention, and he still struggled with doubt and pangs of loneliness. But what he was learning about God did put him on a trajectory. His life turned in a new direction, though he still had a long way to travel in that new direction. What changed was his perspective.

"We come out of the womb wanting gain and profit," Lee says. "But we shortchange ourselves. We go for the things in the world, but they really disappoint. They don't last. They rust, and thieves break in and steal them. We can lose them in a flash in the stock market. What God can offer us is lasting. It's permanent."

At the height of his career, compelled by a divine tugging in his heart, Lee quit his job. He left it all and decided to follow through on a bet he made with God.

"I'm a gambler," he says. "This life is a bet. I can't prove to you there is a God. But life is an all-in bet. I've got all my chips on that one square that says, 'Jesus is King.' I am second because he is first. And all of us who are second will one day be made first when he comes back for us. That's my bet."

Despite his experience in Germany, Lee had lived most of his life like the rest of us. He'd made as much money as he could. He'd bought a nice house and raised a family. He'd worked too much.

"I haven't always had the ability to follow through with the things I wanted to do. I was not a good father. I was interested in making money and wouldn't let anything stop me. I just knew that this was not what life is about. My soul wanted to know more about God."

About the time he realized this, the United Kingdom was about to hand Hong Kong back over to the Chinese. In the hands of British overseers, this peninsular colony had grown from a small fishing village to the third-busiest trading port on earth. But the ninety-nine-year lease the British had held on the port was set to expire. Many Hong Kong Christians feared that the churches that had flourished during these years would be squashed by communist China. So a group of Chinese believers decided to take the church underground to help it survive any coming dangers. Their plan was to take it out of the steepled buildings and into the homes and workplaces of the people.

Lee became intrigued by these Christians—by their mix of love for God and their native country.

"They were patriots," he says. "They loved China. I had always been ashamed to be Chinese. They were ordinary believers who didn't have to function with an institution. They knew how to live out faith in their ordinary lives. They knew how to live attractive lives of faith. I didn't know how to live that life. I had to change. The main benefit of Christianity is the power to change your life."

Lee and Miltinnie spent the next seventeen years of their lives in Hong Kong learning how to live that changed life. They taught the people they met there to do the same. It wasn't about Sunday church, going to mass, or saying a certain prayer. They lived out their faith every day in the workplace—they both worked in secular, nonreligious jobs—in their neighborhood, and with their family.

"I saw how this life is training for the next life," Lee remembers. "When we get this eternal perspective, the things of this world start fading. With Jesus you get the very power of God to change your life. You get a purpose in life."

Lee had made a bet that the purpose of life was not money or comfort, but love. He followed Jesus' teaching that said, "Love your neighbor as yourself." Jesus brought that teaching at the cost of his own life on a cross.

"God paid a big price," Lee says. "He gave his Son to die for us and to take care of that sin problem. I had botched up my life. I botched up my marriage. I was going nowhere in my career in the military. God gave me a second chance. My purpose now is in being second, in humbling myself and taking on the character of Jesus. Even Jesus said he didn't come to be served but to serve and to give his life as a ransom for many. I find purpose in following Jesus in that."

What started as a feeble, lonely prayer to a God he hoped would accept him sent Lee Yih on a lifelong quest to love others as God loved him. He hadn't known love before God, and now he wanted to know nothing else. With every step toward God, the things of this world faded in their importance. He found love, purpose, and a friend in God.

Lee now runs a ministry called Layman's Foundation, a national association of believers who want to use their vocations to represent Jesus in the workplace. They teach people the power of God's love to fill even the loneliest holes in their hearts.

The love of God healed Lee and Miltinnie. It filled their hearts and gave them purpose. And the same all-powerful love changed the lives of the Robertson family. Made famous through a reality television show about their duck-call business, they testify to the power of God to radically change a life and a family.

Chapter 4
Family

sometimes it takes a fight

PHIL AND KAY ROBERTSON, STARS OF A&E'S *DUCK DYNASTY*

You're gonna have to fight for your marriage," her grandmother said as they shucked peas on the front porch of her house in Louisiana.

"Why would I have to fight for my marriage?" Kay asked. Nanny had taught Kay to cook, to believe in God, and to be kind to others. She didn't have much of an education, but she overflowed with the simple wisdom of a woman who had lived life.

"It's going to be like all the books," Kay insisted. "I'm going to have four kids and live happily ever after."

"I know that you feel like that now," Nanny said, "but somewhere in life you're gonna have to fight for your marriage. Remember this: it's one man and one woman for one life."

Kay tried to understand, though fairy tales and romantic novels don't tell about the arguments and the struggles a marriage can bring. She trusted her grandmother. She spent more time with her than with her own parents. Nanny taught her many truths, but the lesson about marriage took a bit of life to comprehend.

"I knew I was going to marry a pioneer man," Kay says, "the kind of guy who could take me across America in a covered wagon. He would be guiding the whole group. He'd protect me all the way. He was a guy who would hunt and fish. I wanted a rugged man."

Kay met Phil Robertson in high school. This came before the beard and shaggy hair. This was before the Duck Commander company and reality television fame. Phil could live off the land. He knew how to hunt, fish, and grow his own food. He loved the satisfaction of going out hungry and coming back with meat for the table.

"For me it was love at first sight," Kay remembers. "But for him, I didn't come near his hunting and fishing. We dated until hunting season came. He decided he had ducks to kill, squirrels to kill, and fish to catch. I was a little too interfering, so he broke up with me."

Shortly afterward, at age fourteen, Kay lost her father to a massive and sudden heart attack. She got off the bus one day to see cars filling her driveway. A neighbor caught her at the bus stop and brought her inside.

"I'm not sure how to tell you this," the neighbor said. "Your father died today."

Phil came to the funeral to be by her side and never left her again. They were together from that moment on. Kay loved that he cared enough to set aside his hunting to be with her.

Kay and Phil dated all through school. Then Kay got pregnant her junior year. She had known that marriage lay in their future, but this altered the timeline.

"Mama said we just needed to take off and get married. I refused to tell Phil's family because I didn't want them to think less of me. They went to church all the time. I had permission from my mom, but he didn't from his parents. We did a hippy wedding."

They didn't have the papers or the preacher—they wouldn't get legally married until four years later—but they loved each other. They went away and made their own promises to each other.

"I gave myself to him, and I vowed I would never have another," Kay says. "It was marriage for life like my grandmother talked about. I was as married as anybody who has ten marriage certificates."

They had love in their new marriage, but they didn't have any money. Phil had been poor his whole life.

"I was raised in a log cabin," Phil says. "Fireplace in one end—that was the heat source. No bathroom, no bathtub, no commode, and no running water. We had a milk cow, a horse or two, and a plow horse. If you wanted to take a bath, you put some water in a washtub and set it out in the sun to warm up a little. Seven children in the household, and each one would jump in that tub of water."

Phil won a football scholarship to Louisiana Tech University. He and Kay and their baby son, Alan, moved to campus and started life together.

"We were basically two kids with a kid," Kay says. "But you have to grow up, and you do."

She started to see a change in Phil after he joined the team. His parents had taken him to church growing up. But now, on his own, he took a different path.

"As soon as I got old enough, sin sprang to life," Phil says. "I went to college and was on my way to being a bone to be chewed. I went on a rebellious run. There was a lot of error."

Phil's football buddies loved to party. None had a wife and child to care for. But Phil did, and he partied the way they did.

"It was scary to me," Kay says. Her mother had been a drinker when Kay was growing up, especially after her father died. Drinking had changed her mother, and Kay watched as it brought out a temper in Phil she didn't want to see.

"I didn't want to be part of it, but I didn't want to lose my husband. I didn't know what to do with that."

Reluctantly, she came to many of the parties. One night, unable to find a babysitter, she brought Alan with her. She put him down for bed in one of the rooms. He ended up getting sick.

"He had thrown up and was running a fever. I got a blanket, wrapped him up, and told Phil that we had to leave."

"I'm not leaving," he said.

"We have to leave. The baby is sick."

"I'm not leaving."

The choice was made. Phil would party. Kay would take care of their boy. It was a terrible arrangement they kept up for years to come.

Kay would make excuses for him. *Those football players had a bad influence on him. If we make it through school, it'll change. He'll stop drinking.* But he didn't. Phil graduated, then got a job teaching and coaching football out of state.

"I was pregnant with Jason by then and we moved to our new place. It was going to be a new life. Phil would be a great family man and just quit drinking. But the drinking got worse. He found new people to party with."

Boy number three, Willie Jess, came along next.

"With Phil having another boy, he's got to think about that," she said to herself. "He's going to slow the partying and drinking down. It's going to get better."

But it only got worse.

"He started carousing around on me," she says. "I knew, but I didn't want to believe it. I had to stay with him because that's what Nanny had told me—one man for one life."

Phil came home one evening with a surprise announcement. He had quit his job at the school and leased out a local bar. He promised to slow down the drinking and focus on making money. They'd save up and then get out of town to something better. Kay just had to tough it out until then.

"I kept thinking about one man, one life—that's what Nanny said. But I didn't want to work in a bar. Do I go with him? What do I do? My only thought was, we'll make the money, then we'll go to somewhere good, and our life will start over. We got a trailer up there by the bar. I was a barmaid who didn't drink and had three little boys."

The drinking never died down during that time, but Phil and Kay did make good money. They stashed away as much as they could. Dreaming of their future life kept Kay's spirit alive. Then, with just months left on the lease, Phil got himself in a bar fight that jeopardized it all. He put two people in the hospital. The police came looking for him.

"Well, I've got to get out of town," he told Kay. "I'm gonna be hiding out in the swamp. I won't surface for two or three months. Do the best you can with what's left here, and then we'll start over somewhere else."

With that, Phil Robertson disappeared into the Louisiana swampland. The pioneer man knew how to win a fight and how to hide from the law. He'd later become famous for playing the hillbilly on reality television.

"Now I understood why my grandmother said you have to fight for your marriage," Kay says. "But I never thought it would be like this."

Kay ransomed Phil from his legal woes with the money they had saved up, the money they had planned to spend on a new life. The people he injured agreed not to press charges if she turned over all she had. She did. They started over, but not the way she had hoped.

"Phil got another job as a roughneck, drilling oil in the bottom of the Gulf [of Mexico]. His drinking was far worse than it ever had been his whole life. He became mean spirited. He was unhappy with himself because he had lost all the money. I would tell my boys all the time that it was the Devil in him. That wasn't their daddy. Don't hate him. Hate the Devil."

Kay came home late from work one night. First the car had given her problems and she had to work on it in the rain. When she finally got it going again she found out that Phil hadn't picked up the youngest from daycare as he had promised, so she had to drive out to get him. She finally fell through the door with all their kids—late, tired, and wet—to find Phil drunk on the couch.

"I know why you were late," he snapped as she came in. "You're having an affair. I know you have somebody else."

"When would I have time to do that?"

"I know you're running around on me."

"He called me bad names," she remembers. And to Kay, that moment was the "lowest point in my whole life. I wouldn't do that. I would never embarrass my children like that. My only goal in life was to be a good wife and a good mother. It was all falling apart."

She ran into the bathroom, closed the door, and cried.

"I just wanted peace," she says. "I wished I could take pills and just go to sleep and never wake up." If she did that, she thought, "Phil would be so hurt and would understand what he had done to me and his family. He would straighten up. That's what I wanted."

At that moment Alan, just shy of ten, came to the door.

"Momma, please don't cry," he said. "It's gonna be all right. God is gonna take care of us."

"I could hear the pitter-patter of all the boys' feet. I'll never forget that sound. It's like a light went on. *Who's going to take care of these three little boys? A drunk sitting on the couch? I'm all they got.* I got on my knees and I prayed."

"God, help me find peace," she prayed. "Help me find some hope. Save my marriage."

She wiped her tears, came out, and told the boys everything would be all right. She got dinner started, turned on the TV, and stared in surprise when she recognized the face of a man on one of the commercials.

Years earlier, a local pastor named Bill Smith had come into their bar carrying a Bible and wanting to tell the people there about Jesus. Phil wasn't having it. He'd run the man out of his bar and told him he didn't want to hear anything he had to say. Now that same Bill Smith was on TV, promising to show people hope. Kay wrote down the phone number and called to arrange a meeting at Bill's church.

"I thought I had a relationship with God," she told Bill when they met. "But I have no hope. I have no peace in my life. Everything around me is falling apart."

"Do you feel like if you died today you would go to heaven?" he asked.

"Yeah. Why not? I have lived with an unlovable man for almost ten years. He's mean-spirited. He ran around on me. But I stayed with him."

"It'll just be you and God," Bill said. "Phil's not going to be with you. Is that what you're going to tell God?"

"He's got to give me credit for all this."

"Let me tell you a story," he said.

Then Bill Smith told Kay the simple story of Jesus. He told

about how all the world had done wrong and fallen away from God. This brought death, pain, and separation between God and his people. To heal the divide and bring forgiveness and life to all, God sent his only Son. This Son, Jesus, came to pay the debt of all the world's wrongs, big and small. He gave his life up on a cross, was buried, and rose again three days later. And anyone who followed after him would have hope, peace, and a new life.

That story struck Kay deep. "I learned Jesus is in heaven right now and he's coming back for me. I put my faith in that. I repented of my sins and confessed him to be the Lord of my life. It was the greatest thing that ever happened to me. I was going to have help. He died on the cross for me. He was buried for me."

Bill warned Kay that coming to Jesus brings hope for the future, not always instant change in the present. In other words, Phil would likely be as mean and drunk as ever when she got home. One day Jesus would come back to fix it all and to wipe away the tears. But until then, in this life, she'd probably have plenty of struggle.

"Just be gentle and love him," he said. "We'll try to visit him. Keep praying."

Bill and others from his church did visit, but Phil never listened. They would come in one door, and he'd run out the other. Meanwhile, Kay and the boys started following hard after Jesus. They joined Bill's congregation and served where they could. They made new friends and built a new life with God and their church.

"My life was changing," she says. "But it was still hard. I had a drunk husband. Phil grew more and more unhappy with me and the boys and our new life. Finally he kicked us all out. 'I'm sick of you,' he said. 'I just can't stand your holy-roller life. I can't stand that you're talking to the boys about God and going to heaven. Everybody's reading their Bibles. You're just ruining my life!'"

Their church helped Kay and the boys move into a low-cost apartment, and they dove deeper into their new church life. If the church doors were open, they were there. But Kay still struggled with sadness. She had prayed for a new life for her family, but it seemed that only part of her prayer had been answered. Yes, she and the boys had found peace and hope. But without Phil, their lives felt incomplete.

"I prayed for a complete family," she says. "I had a big hole in my heart without Phil. The boys were devastated. They missed their dad. I had everybody praying."

One day, she spotted Phil's gray pickup truck outside of her workplace. She went out to talk with him and saw his head leaning over the steering wheel. She couldn't tell if he had passed out drunk or had fallen asleep.

When she walked up, Phil raised his head and looked at her. His eyes, puffy and red, filled with tears.

"I can't eat," he said. "I can't sleep. I want my family back."

"My heart started beating hard," she recalls. "This was just what I wanted and had prayed for. But something inside of me told me to be strong."

"You'll have to change your life," she said.

"I need help."

"I know who can help you."

"You're gonna say God." He shook his head.

"He's the only one who can help you."

"I don't know how to find him."

Kay called up Bill Smith, and they met at the house. Kay took the boys to the store while he and Phil talked. She prayed and prayed. She had hoped for a new life after Phil finished college and after each of the boys were born. She'd longed for it when they moved and when they leased the bar. But all she had experienced was disappointment. Could this be different? She dared to hope.

Meanwhile, Bill was asking Phil a pointed question: "What do you think the gospel is?"

"I didn't have any idea," Phil recalls saying. "I don't know how I had missed it. I grew up in church. I don't know whether they weren't teaching it or whether I was just blinded by the evil one, but I had missed it. Bill went through Jesus coming down in flesh, dying on a cross for my sins, being buried and raised from the dead. How in the world did I ever miss that? I was blown away when I heard that Jesus died for me."

Kay came back with the boys to find a note on the door. Phil and Bill had gone to the church building. The boys were overjoyed. "What if the Devil is really gonna leave daddy this time?" they said. "What if he's gonna be nice again and go to church with us?"

Kay could hardly breathe. A lump formed in her throat as she threw the boys back in the car and raced to the church. They found Phil standing in the baptistry with Bill's arm around him.

"I want to make Jesus the Lord of my life," they heard him say as they walked in. "I want to follow him from this day forward. I don't ever want to live the life I've lived before. I want to be a good man. I want to be a good father. I want to be a good husband."

"For the first twenty-eight years of my life," Phil says, recalling this moment, "I had no idea who Jesus was. It's only when you meet Jesus and you look back at where you were, you end up saying, 'What was I thinking?' I have found the rarest of commodities, peace of mind. I never had that the first twenty-eight years."

Kay and the boys watched their husband and father go down into the water and rise again a new man. All his life, he had lived only for himself. But that was about to change.

"I didn't even know what love was," Phil says. "I went from getting commode-hugging drunk, leading a life of misery, to meeting Jesus. Once I was baptized, I came out thinking, *I'm going to be as wide open for good and for God as I was for the evil one and living this sinful lifestyle.*"

"I looked down at each one of the boys," Kay says. "Tears were rolling down their faces. Even three-year-old Willie Jess had big tears coming down. When Phil came up out of the water, the boys started hollering and singing, jumping all over the place. They were so happy. It was the complete family."

"I looked up to heaven and told my Nanny, 'Well, I did fight for my marriage. And guess what? I still have it.'"

"I'm fixing to make a valiant attempt to be good," Phil told her. "I never tried it before." But he's been trying ever since. "Bill told me to love God and love your neighbor. So I do. I try to love people now and tell everybody I can about this Jesus."

Phil soon learned that loving his wife and boys came easier

than loving some other people—especially when someone started stealing his catfish.

By that time, Phil had turned his knack for hunting ducks into a company that sold duck calls. But Duck Commander had made only eight thousand dollars in sales in its first year. While he grew the business, Phil paid the bills by catching catfish and selling them for thirty cents a pound. It was the only way he knew to pay the bills and make ends meet. So he was not at all happy when someone started stealing the fish out of his nets.

"It was my livelihood," he remembers. "I had to survive and feed my children. I'd caught several of the thieves before then. I was going to catch them again."

Usually, this involved some nasty words and a shotgun. But now Phil had decided to follow Jesus, and that complicated matters. He read in the Bible that Jesus said to love your enemies, to pray for those who persecute you. "I was thinking that didn't make a whole lot of sense. They were stealing my fish! But God just told me to be good to them and not return evil for evil—if they were hungry, to feed them. I decided to see if that would work."

Catfish feed along the river bottoms. To catch them in any quantity, you have to rig up a deep net and trap them, almost as you would catch lobster or crab. The net is attached to a line with a floatation device at the surface. One day while out checking his nets, Phil spotted the thieves boating toward one of them. He scooted his boat into the weeds along the shore to watch them. The moment he saw them start to pull up his net, he started his motor.

"Usually, I would scare them off at the point of a gun," he says. "But Jesus had told me to love them and I decided I'm going to follow Jesus. I asked what they were doing, and they lied to me at first, saying they were just fishing. I told 'em I had good news for them. They could have any fish I had in my trap."

At first, the thieves didn't believe Phil. But he insisted. They brought their boat up alongside his while he pulled up the trap. It was filled with catfish.

"Whoa! Pretty good catch," he said. "Look what you boys were fixin' to get. But have no fear. I'm gonna give 'em to you."

He proceeded to toss all the fish from the net into their boat. Then he started throwing even more fish toward them. He gave them fish from other traps he'd pulled up earlier that day. Finally they refused to take any more fish. But Phil wouldn't take no for an answer.

"You start frying fish," he told them, "and kinsfolk will show up that you never even heard of before. Let's make sure you have enough."

And he kept throwing fish into his enemies' boat.

And after that day, "all of a sudden, up and down the river, they quit stealing my fish," he says. "It didn't make earthly sense."

But Jesus proved right.

Jesus gives a better life. His path doesn't always run straight. His instructions don't always make sense to us. But he heals families. He restores marriages. He fixes what nobody else can put back together. He doesn't do it all by himself, of course. He brings us along for the struggle. He'll tie the gloves to our hands, lift our arms, and push us into the ring.

"I'm here for you," he shouts from the corner. "I'm not going to let you fall."

FAMILY

You'll take some punches in this life. That's a given. But hope comes from knowing who's in your corner. He'll tag in when you go down. He'll refresh you when you grow weary. You'll hear his voice shouting your name through the worst of it. You'll need to fight for your family, for your marriage, and for all the good things in this life. But with Jesus you'll fight with the knowledge that if he is for you, no one can be against you.

Finding Peace in Identity and Purpose

People tend to pin who they are on what they do and on what people think of what they do. This is true whether a person works for pay or works at home caring for a family. Identity gets tied to activity. We think we are what we do. And the better we do it, the better version of ourselves we think we become.

But this kind of thinking leads either to a despairing perfectionism or a sense of pointlessness. At some point we'll look down that ladder and find we're no happier where we are now than we were at the bottom. Society tends to applaud architects more than waiters, so we assume that a better career will give life more meaning. But careers can fall as fast as they rise, so they are poor foundations for any lasting peace.

Sometimes we think that if we could just perfect our work—or at least the image of our work that others have of it—then maybe we could finally quiet the storms of doubt in our heads. But that's a false hope too. There is no perfecting our work because there is no perfecting us.

Finding peace in identity and purpose means finding something deeper than work to base it all on. We have to find a truth and a reality that go beyond what we do or how we present ourselves to the world. We have to find an identity that gives meaning to our activity, not the other way around. And we definitely need a purpose higher than the opinions and likes of others.

These are the stories of people who found this deeper identity and higher purpose and, in the process, found the peace that comes with it.

Chapter 5
Control

why I gave it up

BEN KING, PROFESSIONAL CYCLIST

If your yardstick for success is "better than the others," then you will find you don't measure up for long. Records never last, and winners don't stay on top forever. Perfection will always evade capture. There is always someone better. Peace can't be won by victory.

Maybe you've heard the old story about the sun and the wind. They made a bet about who could get a certain man to take off his coat. The wind blew his hardest, but the man only wrapped the coat more tightly around him. The more the wind blew, the tighter the man's grip. But when the sun simply smiled, the man gladly removed his coat in the warmth.

You can't get peace by outmuscling another. You can't earn it. You can't demand it. Peace is letting go, not holding on. Peace is trust, not control. It's setting yourself free from comparisons. No story illustrates this simple truth more clearly than that of professional cyclist Ben King. Ben embodies grit and determination. For years he thrived on four-a-day training sessions, a diet mastered to the cellular level, and just pure raw drive. But none of that won him the peace he sought.

Ben King burns more energy in one day than you or I might in four days. For every step we might take, he takes four. For every mile the average person might go, he goes another three. "Whether it's snowing or raining and cold, I still go out and do five- or six-hour rides," he says. "Suffering becomes a lifestyle. You have to embrace it."

And all that's just the prelude to the real challenge: race day.

"You're bumping elbows, bumping handlebars, and you don't get to determine the pace. The pace is set for you. It's like getting pulled along on a choke collar. I can remember certain races when I was actively looking for a safe place to crash. The race was that hard. We're just getting sprayed in the face with cow manure that's fallen out of trucks on these little tiny roads. Other riders are elbowing you off the road, but there's nowhere to go but a ditch and barbed wire. It's grueling."

There's a science to cycling too. The formulaic dynamics of weight and the power needed to carry that weight determine everything. The numbers tell competitive cyclists what to eat and how to train. Every pound of flesh is a pound that has to be carried on the bike. Every calorie eaten is a calorie that needs to be burned.

"Everything in this sport is extremely calculated," Ben explains. "We measure our energy expenditure with a power meter that tells us how many calories we burn, what kind of intensity the workout was. That's all relayed back to a coach who can analyze the micro and macro cycles of your training. I'll burn five or six thousand extra calories a day in training, and that means eating eight thousand calories."

The world's most grueling races require equally grueling training. Ben would one day win his way into the famous Tour de France at the age of twenty-five. But training to achieve those heights started in high school and continued through to college. It meant beginning every day for years on a bike at six in the morning. It meant lifting weights at school and then practicing track after school. Then came homework, dinner, and swim practice, only to begin it all again the next day. And there came a time when the constant striving for that perfect training edge almost broke him down physically, mentally, and spiritually.

"I got to the point where I couldn't train any more than I was," he says. "But I still felt like if I wasn't taking advantage of every minute of free time in my day, that I wasn't doing my best."

Since Ben couldn't physically train any more, he looked for other things he could control, like his diet. In his mind, he let in too many calories, failed to control every bite or to check every caloric cheat. But the massive calorie-demanding workouts came with equally demanding cravings.

"One night, I came home, and I started to write an essay at the kitchen counter. There was a big loaf of French bread on the counter with olive oil and vinegar."

As he wrote the paper, he started ripping chunks of bread off the loaf and dipping them in oil. He mindlessly ate piece after piece until finally his hand grasped at an empty plate.

"I looked at the bag. Two thousand calories of bread I just ate. Then I went and sat down at dinner and had two giant plates of pasta and chicken for dinner. I was disgusted with myself and felt like I'd lost self-control, even though I knew that's what my body needed. I was trying to deny my body what it needed in order to control my weight and my performance."

He ran outside, despairing the loss of control. He had calculated everything so carefully for so long. A loaf of bread and a couple of plates of pasta had ruined all the precision.

"I was just broken," he says. "I was totally exhausted. I looked off into the woods. I tried to pray, but there was just this white noise in my brain."

Frustrated, desperate for control, needing to undo his earlier moment of weakness, he made himself throw up.

"This was my twisted way to regain control," he says. "I knew it was unhealthy. I was ashamed."

And yet that one-time event devolved into a regular part of Ben's diet. He purged whenever he needed to feel control. The frequent vomiting eventually tore his esophagus, pouring blood in his vomit. The limitations of his body stared back at him in red whenever he threw up. The physical strain began eroding his emotional and mental well-being as well.

"My mom had me do dishes one night," he says. "I was washing the dishes roughly, and I broke a salad bowl that my mom really liked. She got angry with me for being reckless with the dishes, and rightfully so. But I lost my temper and ran out the door.

"I had been totally beating my body into submission. But the thing I was trying to control was beginning to control me. I was training three or four times a day and had been purging every time I felt like I had overeaten."

He ran aimlessly into the woods that night in a confused and manic mental state.

"It was just this weird moment where all the trees overhead and the branches were making these eerie gestures at me. I felt like I was surround by this evil presence. It may just have been the evil I had allowed into my life. I yelled into the night, 'Do something or go back to hell!'"

No answer.

Ben found a log in the woods and lay down. He spent the night under the stars in a restless sleep. "I had never had an outburst like that," he remembers. "I didn't know how to react to it."

The next day his father came up to his room to talk with him.

"I was ashamed," Ben says. "He asked me what was going on, and I knew he would have been understanding, but I didn't want anyone to know. I kept it from him. But he prayed with me."

"God," his father prayed, "we pray that you would just take this. We would acknowledge that you are in control of everything."

"That's when I realized what I was doing," Ben says. "Not only was I hurting myself, dishonoring God, but I was hurting the people around me, the people that I loved and cared about.

"There's a verse in the Bible that really spoke to me through all this.[1] It talks about how our bodies aren't capable of perfection, but God is still in control. There's a promise that I will someday have a new body. I realized that there were things in my life that

I couldn't control. I decided to trust God with those things, and then they no longer controlled me. I didn't have to deal with the anxiety and the pressure to perform. I was free to compete without needing to earn love, value, or acceptance. I was free to compete because I'm already loved and valued."

In 2010, Ben King became the youngest-ever winner of the USA Cycling Pro Championship race. He went on to compete in the famed Tour de France and in numerous world championships.

"I've experienced way more than I ever could have dreamed of with this sport," he says. "But I've learned to depend on God and his promises that he'll control the things that I can't, that he's faithful. I was really unhealthy. Striving for perfection broke me down. It was unsustainable. But with this new perspective, cycling has brought me a lot of joy. It's an act of worship. I have a lot more pressure on my shoulders now that I've gone professional, but God is in control."

Ben King's story is one of extremes: constant training, crazy diet, elite races. But through it all he found a peace in letting go. He found peace in releasing control, not in holding on to it.

Life is filled with the unknown, the scary, and the uncontrollable. Perfection will elude each of us. We can never have sufficient control of ourselves, of our world, or of those around us to guarantee the results we seek. We will then either be consumed by the chaos or forced to trust the God who holds the chaos in his hands.

Bestselling author Eric Metaxas found himself at a similar crossroad while working a proofreading job. Life proved frustrating and seemed pointless. He needed to hear from God. He needed God to give him a purpose and a mission. But did God even exist? And if he did, did he care about a lowly proofreader working a boring corporate job?

Chapter 6
Thinker

when God speaks through a fish

ERIC METAXAS, AUTHOR AND SPEAKER

I felt like I was in a dark room made of Sheetrock," Eric Metaxas says. "There's no window. There's no door. There's no way out. Unless God punches a hole through the Sheetrock and reveals himself from the other side, then I'm just trapped. I'm trapped in my own mind, in my own way of seeing the world."

Eric sought a God he wasn't sure existed. He sought an answer to a question he didn't know could even be answered. A self-described bookish kid who went on to study literature at Yale, Eric found solace in humanity's long wrestling match with this singular question.

"With the great minds of history, philosophers and writers," he says, "you see the question: What is the meaning of life?

You see through the great literature of the Western canon this one idea."

Despite growing up in the Greek Orthodox Church, Eric never found the answer in that tradition. Church, for him, never rose above a social gathering place or an ethnic community center.

"It was religion in the negative sense," he says. "I never learned about the Christian faith. I did not reject God. I believed in him. But our church was mainly built on the idea of being Greek. It's where the Greeks hung out. It was an ethnic community, not a community of faith. You just went to church. You didn't know why you believed what you believed. You didn't even know whether you believed it."

The son of immigrant parents, Eric clung close to his ethnic identity while growing up. He identified as the smart Greek kid, someone who studied, read, and asked big questions of life.

"I could read when I was four," he says. "I skipped first grade. I always got good grades in school. It became my identity, being the smart kid."

Born in New York but raised in a small town in Connecticut for much of his youth, Eric didn't know many people who shared his academic interests. His parents had never graduated from college. His friends mostly enjoyed fishing and the outdoors. But despite his surroundings, his love for learning and literature propelled him to one of the nation's top schools.

"At Yale I began discovering who I was," Eric says. "I went to college not really knowing what I believed. Yale is a very secular environment, and it did not take long for most of my faith to evaporate and go underground to where it didn't mean anything. By the time I graduated I was absolutely at sea. But I joined the *Yale Record*, which is the world's oldest college humor magazine, and later became the editor. There I realized this is what I love: literature, ideas, writing."

Eric finished Yale as an English major with a desire to write, but he struggled to find a career that matched the desire. "I graduated not knowing how to become a writer," he says. "What does that even mean? What did I want to write? How do I do that? There's no path. It's not like medical school or banking. There's just no path. I floundered. I drifted."

Eric's search for life's great answer still dogged his mind. Eventually he settled upon a sort of answer—or at least a path toward the answer. It pointed the way but didn't bring him to the destination. His answer came in the form of a picture.

"I came up with what I thought was a suitable answer to the meaning of the universe," he says. "I came up with this literary image. You have a frozen lake. The ice on the lake represents the conscious mind. The water beneath the ice represents the unconscious mind or the collective unconscious—Carl Jung's idea of God, this kind of Eastern God-force. So, the goal of life and of all religions is basically the same. It's to drill through the ice, the conscious mind, to reach the collective unconscious, this God-force. This was what all religions were really getting at. That's what I thought, at the time."

Reading Carl Jung may seem like torture to some people, but immersing himself in this esoteric thinker gave Eric a sense of clarity. While Jung couldn't promise an answer through any specific religion, Eric thought he could show how all religions basically get people to dig for this "God," who is revealed deep within a person. Jung taught that you could touch God if only you could drill down deep enough within your own unconscious mind. This "God" wasn't personal or active, but he was in there somewhere. Life, then, if spent drilling for God, would yield its purpose. It was just a matter of getting through the ice.

Unfortunately, developing philosophically complex literary images doesn't pay the bills. Eric ended up doing what many do after college. He moved back in with his parents. His immigrant parents had high aspirations for their son. They hoped he would reach higher heights than they had in their new country. This expectation compounded when their son attended and then graduated from an elite college. For Eric to struggle to find a job and then move back home strained their relationship.

"But they didn't know how to advise me," he remembers. "They never had the experience of this kind of thing. So we were at an impasse in our relationship."

With pressure mounting, Eric took a position at Union Carbide, a chemical and polymers company. He worked as a proofreader for company publications—not exactly high-minded literature.

"To work in a corporate environment," he says, "when you think of yourself as a humorist, a poet, a writer, was horrible. It was a really unpleasant, awful time. But there was nothing I could do. I'm living at home, miserable, working this awful job, not knowing how to become a writer. There was a lot of depression. I had no answers."

While at Union Carbide, Eric made a friend, Ed Tuttle, who worked there as a graphic designer. Years earlier Ed had had a profound experience with God. He hadn't been looking for God or asking God to show up. But out of nowhere, God had appeared to Ed, visible and tangible. That moment transformed Ed Tuttle from a jaded doubter into a rabid believer. He carried this into his relationship with Eric.

"He clearly was serious about his Christian faith," Eric remembers. "For a long time, that made me uncomfortable. I had been trained at Yale. We avoided people like this. *These are weird people.* But I was in enough pain to put those feelings aside, and I learned a lot talking to him. There was no way I'd accept what he was saying. I just asked more questions, and a lot of my intellectual objections were removed. This was a long process, months of confusion."

In the middle of these many conversations, Ed challenged Eric to pray.

"You should pray," Ed said. "Pray that God would reveal himself to you."

"I remember thinking that made absolutely no sense," Eric says. "I didn't even know if God was there. How was I going to pray to him? I didn't even know if he existed. But if you're in enough pain, you'll do stupid stuff."

Disgruntled with his job proofreading corporate publications, frustrated with living at home, and still struggling to find the meaning of life, Eric succumbed to Ed's challenge. He began to pray for God to speak, to punch up through the ice. Eric couldn't find a way through the ice on his own. He couldn't even be sure that if he got through the ice God would be there. And if God was there, did he care about people or about him specifically? Or was he just some vague energy force, like in *Star Wars*? Would such a God even be worth digging for?

"I continued to pray intermittently," he says. "I'm just in pain. I'm not happy with my folks. I'm living at home. Did I say how awful my job was? Then my uncle had a stroke."

He told Ed about his uncle, and Ed's response shocked him.

"Ed said to me that some of the folks at his church were praying for my uncle. I'll never forget that. I was blown away by the kindness of this. These people didn't even know my uncle. These people didn't even know me. But they were praying for my uncle."

"I was also blown away by the intellectual concept that they were praying to this God they thought could heal people. To them God was not just some vague energy force. They actually believed there was this God who cares. I wasn't persuaded that this was real, but I was moved by the concept of it."

"Would you like to pray for your uncle?" Ed then asked Eric.

"Up until then, I would have said, 'no way,'" Eric says. "I didn't want to do anything weird. I didn't want to go to church or do Bible study."

Intellectually, Eric had run to the end of the road. No religion could give definitive proof of God. Philosophy told him to dig for God but left him completely unequipped to actually conduct the search successfully. He needed God in order to find any meaning in life, but he couldn't find God unless God came out of hiding.

Out of logical options, he then went for the illogical.

"Ed took me into this bleak, florescent-lit conference room

at Union Carbide," he says. "We closed the door. He prayed. I closed my eyes. I had never done this before, ever. I grew up in the church. I was an altar boy. But nobody prayed, actually prayed, like this.

"After Yale, I only wanted to hang out with the cool people. I wanted to be around people who smoked clove cigarettes and read French poetry. I didn't want to hang out with crazy religious people. It was pure prejudice, but that's where I was. I thought if there was a truth, it had to be larger than that weird Christian stuff, something broader that incorporates all religions. It was this visceral sense that I didn't like those people. It really had nothing to do with actually wrestling with the ideas.

"I found out through Ed that I really didn't know much of anything about the Christian faith. I was ashamed at how little I actually knew. I realized I had picked up this cartoon version of Christian faith that didn't have any bearing on reality."

Eric's uncle died despite the prayers, but the experience of talking with a God who might care and who could have answered stuck with him.

"It wasn't like a big mystical thing," he says. "But when I opened my eyes, I realized this is real. A window opened up into eternity. I could feel this faint breeze from someplace else. On an intellectual level, I knew I needed God. I needed God to reveal himself to me. My brain is a dead end. I couldn't go any farther. We can't know these things on our own. We can't get to heaven with our brains. Unless God reached out to me, then I was stuck. I needed a miracle, but I was not expecting him to do a miracle."

Soon afterward, Eric had a dream that toppled this last impediment. In his dream he stood on a lake in Danbury, Connecticut, where he grew up.

"It's winter. I'm standing on the ice. I'm ice fishing with my buddy John and his dad. It's one of those glorious winter days where the sun is bright and the sky is incredibly blue. There's white snow and ice."

He looked down into the fishing hole, and a fish stuck its snout into the air. Fish don't typically come to the surface to let you grab them, but this one did.

"In the dream, it happened. I reached down, and I picked it up. It was a bronze-colored fish. The light from the sun shone so bright that it looked golden. Suddenly I realized that it didn't just look gold; it was actually golden. I was holding a living golden fish, like something out of a fairy tale.

"With that, it's like these paragraphs just dropped into my head. This dream may not have meant anything to anyone else, but I knew God had just one-upped me with my own symbol system. It was like he'd just said to me in my dream, without a word, 'Eric, you wanted to touch water, inert water, this collective unconsciousness, but I have something else for you. I have my Son, Jesus Christ, your Savior.'"

God had spoken using the very symbolism with which Eric had defined the universe. He took Eric's idea of a sheet of ice separating the conscious mind from God, and he punched a hole through that ice. God answered Eric in exactly the way Eric needed. But it wasn't just God breaking through the ice that shocked Eric so much but what came through the hole in the ice. He expected inert water—some vague, nonpersonal, godlike energy. But what came through was a living, golden, fish.

"When those chrome fishes started popping up on the bumpers of cars, my father had gotten really excited, telling me they represented a Greek word. Christians came up with the fish symbol before the cross became the popular symbol. The Greek word for *fish* was used as an acronym which in the Greek language meant, 'Jesus Christ, the Son of God, our Savior.'

"In my dream, I instantly knew all this came together. It just blew my mind. I'm holding this fish, and this fish is Jesus Christ, the Son of God."

He could raise no more objections, give no more denials. Try as he might, he had been unable to find a way through the ice. He'd come to the point where one option was left—a crazy, religious-nut-type option. God would have to come through the ice and speak to him. The God of the universe would have to break through the ice and call his name.

"When he did, I knew my search was over," Eric says. "I didn't know if you could know God, but suddenly I realized he was real. This was true. I was flooded with joy knowing that. Jesus had come from the other side. I had him. I was holding him. He was mine. It was transcendent."

He went to work the next day and told his friend Ed about his dream.

"Well, what do you think that means?" Ed asked.

"What I said next I never, never would have said," Eric says. "I would have cringed to say these words. In fact, I would have cringed if anybody else said those words. I always cringed when people said stuff like this. But here I was saying it, because it was true."

"It means I've accepted Jesus," Eric responded.

"It totally changed everything. It was like going to sleep single and waking up married. I didn't ask for this to happen, but it happened. My life was changed. Now all I had to do was unpack it, lean into it, experience it. But there was no going back.

"I suddenly had the key to the universe, the key to my life. If there was a God who knew me intimately and loved me, then I could trust him. I could give him the rest of my life. I had not been handling life so well, so maybe it would be good for him to try for a while. I was wise enough to know that I was foolish and had no idea what to do next. But I figure that if God makes you, then he knows what gifts he's given you and what you're capable of."

From that day forward, Eric Metaxas let God set the path in his life. Rarely did that path go the way he thought it would. But now he knew he had tapped into the God who had made and designed him, the God who had planned the universe and written his story. He knew that whatever his path, this God knew how best to walk it.

"I turned over my life," he says. "I gave him my career, my writing. He had me figured out. There's so much freedom in that. When God came into my life, I realized I could radically give him everything. He's been my guide in my career. It's the only way to live. We are meant to know that life is not a mistake, that life is not meaningless."

In 2010, Eric Metaxas authored his breakthrough *New York*

Times bestselling book, *Bonhoeffer: Pastor, Martyr, Prophet, Spy*. He followed that book with other bestselling biographies, including *Seven Men: And the Secret of Their Greatness, Seven Women: And the Secret of Their Greatness,* and *Martin Luther: The Man Who Rediscovered God and Changed the World.* He also began hosting a daily, nationally syndicated radio program, *The Eric Metaxas Show,* and founded the New York City event series called "Socrates in the City: Conversations on the Examined Life."

Eric Metaxas now spends his considerable talent telling the stories of people who discovered God's world-altering plan for their lives. Frequently, the heroes of these stories doubt and wonder whether they had any great part to play in the world.

God makes no mistakes. He has a plan for each of his creations, you included. Your inner voice may have doubts or nasty opinions of yourself. But when you know God has you, you find a counter to even the worst of these voices. If God claims you, then you have value and purpose, no matter how you or others view you. God has a plan for your life. It may not be the plan you have, but it is a great plan.

Knowing that God has a plan for your life can bring its own kind of worry. What if you fail to live up to God's plan? What if you just don't turn out to be good enough to live up to his expectations? Olympian Shawn Johnson believed God's plan for her life was Olympic gold. She spent her whole life following this clear mission she believed God had for her life.

What happens if she gets silver instead of gold?

Chapter 7
Perfect

the beauty of failure

SHAWN JOHNSON, OLYMPIC GYMNAST

The search for peace through perfectionism tempts many of us. It shows up in our sixty-hour work weeks, in our manicured social-media posts, even in our fashion choices. It's that obsession to show the world we've got it all together. But peace doesn't come by proving we're perfect but by admitting we're not. Gymnast Shawn Johnson learned this lesson in her journey to Olympic fame.

The road to the Olympics is no smooth ride. From the outside, people might think these elite athletes are just born into this world with an unalterable destiny. But natural talent just gets you on the bike; it doesn't get you up the mountain. Shawn Johnson would one day find herself on the top of that mountain, but it took her more than talent to get there.

"I started gymnastics when I was three years old," she says. "My parents put me in it because I was this rambunctious kid, always jumping off the entertainment centers, doing crazy things. But I quickly fell in love with the sport."

When Shawn was six, her hobby turned more serious. A premier gymnast named Liang Chow moved from Beijing, China, to Shawn's hometown of West Des Moines, Iowa, and started Chow's Gymnastics and Dance Institute. He hoped to find and cultivate young talent into the top ranks of the sport. And he founded that talent in Shawn Johnson.

"When I first met Chow, it wasn't this magical moment," Shawn remembers. "He was like this big kid. He just loved gymnastics, and he wanted his gymnasts to love the sport as much as he did. We joined his gym for budgeting reasons. Chow's gym was closer, and that meant we saved money on gas. But he believed in me, even more than I believed in myself. I never really thought the Olympics were possible. It was my dream, but I never looked at myself and saw an Olympian. That's the difference between me and him."

Chow saw something unique in Shawn—not just talent but also a true love for the sport. Soon going to Chow's gym, practicing and learning the sport, took over Shawn's life—and she began to think that the Olympics really might be in her future.

"I remember watching the Olympics and fantasizing over the career and that lifestyle," she says. "I had such a joy and a love for gymnastics. It led me toward that path. It became my life's dream to wear the red, white, and blue leotard. The one thing that I worked for harder than anything else was that leotard.

It was like a soldier and their uniform. It was symbolic of the journey and the dream. I wanted it more than anything else in the world.

"The gym became my second home," she says. "Committing to the Olympic journey for all those years came from a genuine love for the sport. I genuinely wanted to go back every day. I loved the challenge, the confidence gymnastics gave me. Chow's love of the sport was contagious. I loved being able to work for respect, to earn it. As it got harder over the years, it was more of a sacrifice, more of a struggle, but the sacrifice was never enough that I wanted to quit."

Shawn invested everything into making her dream a reality, as did her parents.

"My parents mortgaged their house," she says. "They never missed a meet, ever. They traveled around the entire world to see me, even when they couldn't afford it. They basically gave up their only child to a different family. In my mind and my heart, the only way that I could repay them was to win gold."

The commitment and sacrifice required to reach the top in gymnastics is unique to the sporting world. No other sport requires so much from athletes so young. Elite gymnasts peak at fourteen or fifteen years old or even younger. To make it in the sport, then, requires an adult-sized commitment from a child.

"It seems very dramatic," she says, "but gymnastics is probably the most brutal sport. It's the only elite-level sport that's dealing with kids. At twelve years old I was traveling the world without my parents and training forty hours a week in a gym. There are football players out there and track athletes who might put in eighty hours a week, but they're not twelve years old. Gymnastics requires that mental strength from a kid."

Combining raw talent, passion, and determination, Shawn gained a place on the 2007 USA Gymnastics senior team and the right to wear her country's colors in international competitions.

"They don't give you your leotard when you first qualify," she says. "It's when you're given the first assignment. That means when you're flying somewhere in the world to compete, they send it to you. It felt like an eternity before the leotards showed up. It was a big box, not glamorous at all. It wasn't in cool wrapping or anything, but the leotards all had the USA emblem on them. I wasn't even at the Olympics yet. But just getting that leotard was validation that what I was doing was working."

She soon proved her worth to USA Gymnastics. In 2007 Shawn Johnson won the much-coveted gold in the all-around event at the American Cup. She brought in gold for the all-around, floor exercise, and balance beam at the Visa National Championships, then proceeded to the Pan American Games, where she again won gold in the all-around, plus the uneven bars, balance beam, and the team gold. She repeated this again at the World Championships, the top competition outside the Olympics, where she won gold with her team, on floor, and all-around.

In 2008, an Olympic year, Shawn continued to shine. Although she dropped to silver in the all-around event at the American Cup, she did win gold in the vault, balance beam, and floor exercise. She won the Visa National Championship and placed first in the all-around at an international competition in Jesolo, Italy. Two weeks later Shawn won the all-around at the US Olympic trials in Philadelphia, securing for herself a spot on the 2008 USA Olympic gymnastics team.

Not surprisingly, by this point, all the accolades had begun to color Shawn's sense of identity. "At sixteen," she remembers, "my identity was entirely about being a gymnast. Every single person in my life had a connection to gymnastics. It was my parents giving up their dreams and money to see me be a gymnast. It was my coaches pushing me and investing their time. I would go to school, and every single person would be asking about gymnastics. All anybody ever wanted to talk about was my life as a gymnast. I didn't have a care in the world except for gymnastics. I didn't have any other space in me that wasn't filled by my sport.

"That obsession is part of what let me compete at an elite level. You can't really be an elite-level athlete without letting something consume you. But there was a negative side."

The same passion and obsession that propelled Shawn to stardom took a toll on her soul, on her identity and self-worth. "I had defined myself as a gymnast," she says. "I found my worth in gymnastics. I found my self-confidence and my pride, my place in this world as a gymnast. I wouldn't know what to do without it."

This sixteen-year-old girl's earliest memories had involved a gym. She had known almost nothing else. And since the age of six, every moment, every dream, every thought had aimed her life toward this competition. In a sport that makes no accommodations to age, the 2008 Beijing Olympics were her best, if not her only, shot at achieving her prize. With the pressure mounting to maintain her sense of worth and meet the world's expectations to win, win, win, she set out for Beijing.

"I was the one to beat and the reigning World Champion going into the Olympics," Shawn remembers. "Every single person and their mother applauded but also critiqued me. I was on a world stage now. Every news article said that I was going to come home with four Olympic gold medals. My big event was the all-around competition."

The all-around competition matches the world's greatest gymnasts against each other in a combined event involving vault, uneven bars, balance beam, and floor exercise. While each athlete is competing for their country, competitors see gold in the all-around as the pinnacle achievement for the individual gymnast. The all-around winner goes down in history as the greatest gymnast on the planet.

Shawn went into each element of the competition with her signature energy and power. But in the vault she stepped one foot forward in the landing—one slight flaw in an otherwise perfect routine. She missed perfection again on the beam, with another stumble in the landing. But with the floor exercise still to come, she held on to hope.

"I looked at all the scores," she says. "I knew the math and realized that if all the girls gave a good floor routine and I gave a great routine, then I could still win the gold medal."

Shawn watched as each gymnast performed her final routine and their scores were posted. There is a maximum number of points available for each routine, based on the routine's unique combination of elements and their difficulty. Even with a perfect routine, a gymnast can't score more than that maximum, but mistakes can bring the scores down below the maximum.

PERFECT

That happened for one competitor after another, keeping Shawn's hope for gold alive.

Then teammate Nastia Liukin came to the mat. Nastia had trailed Shawn throughout the year's competitions. Shawn wrestled with mixed feelings as she watched her prepare. "She's representing the USA," Shawn says. "We are on the same team. I want her to do great, but I also want to do better."

Nastia did her routine with near perfection. The strength of the performance worried Shawn as she took her own place on the mat. She would be the last to perform. It all depended on Nastia's score. If she pulled ahead of Shawn by more than Shawn's maximum, Shawn's chances for gold would end before she even began her routine.

"There's a big scoreboard on the corner of the floor," she remembers. "It has a green light that comes on that gives you thirty seconds to start your routine. But it also shows the other competitors' scores. And just as the green light flashes, Nastia's score comes up."

Shawn's heart sank as she took in the numbers and realized what they meant. Nastia's routine had racked up an impressive 15.525 on floor exercise. That score secured gold for Nastia Liukin. Even Shawn's maximum possible score couldn't win her the long-sought-after medal.

"I'm standing there with thirty seconds left on the clock," she says, "and I'm told in that moment by that score that it was impossible for me to get a gold medal."

In that moment, all of Shawn's dreams seemed to crash down around her. Those years of hard work, the sacrifices made by her parents and coaches—all of it flashed through her mind. She couldn't help but feel the weight of her debt.

"The Olympics are televised live," she remembers. "I know the entire world is being told that I can no longer achieve what they want. I can't win gold. So do I even compete? Do I just throw it? Do I just sit down and cry? I don't know how to act."

The turmoil Shawn felt was completely hidden from the television audience. To the world it looked like a mere pause before her otherwise strong performance on the floor exercise. Despite the assured loss to Nastia, Shawn nailed her routine and won silver in the all-around competition.

Despite winning three silver medals plus a gold on balance beam, Shawn Johnson left the 2008 Olympics devastated. Anything but gold in the all-around competition felt like she had failed to pay back what her parents and so many others had so freely given her.

"The entire world said I would win gold, and I ended up with silver. I'd given 200 percent that day and felt like I had failed the world. I tried to convince myself for years that I was fine with silver. But I wasn't. I felt like I let them down, like I had hit a brick wall. All these people invested all this into me, into my career and my sport, and now it was over. My whole identity was based on gymnastics. I didn't have anything else. And now it was all gone.

"There was this void," she says. "I felt this loss and pain. I'd seen my parents sell their house and move into an apartment, do everything for this dream. There was nothing I could do to repay them. You can't pay people back for their kindness. I don't think there's any payment that will ever be enough. But I somehow thought gold would do it."

The drive to pay back what couldn't be paid grew in her mind until finally she decided to try again in the 2012 London Olympics.

"I set my sights on London," she says. "I went back into the sport with a vengeance. But as soon as I started, I started to decline as well." Old injuries reared their heads, and age took its toll. Most sports reward athletes as they pass into adulthood, but gymnastics only rewards the very young.

"I wasn't sixteen anymore," she says. "I wasn't the perfect image of what the USA national team wanted. I was constantly trying to lose weight and look a certain way, but it wasn't happening. I wasn't able to look like a child. I was just struggling."

Despite the challenges, Shawn's popularity grew. She felt past her prime physically, but the world still hoped for greatness.

"I was signing on Fortune 500 company sponsors," she says. "I was endorsed by Coca-Cola, Nike, Procter & Gamble, and CoverGirl. They were signing up to invest in my Olympic journey—telling me they believed in my journey, in me."

The pressure to win mounted even higher than before.

"For months I pushed myself," she says. "I tried to make my sponsors happy, my parents happy, my coach happy, my team happy. But day after day I would come home from practice just bawling and bawling, just not having any outlet that gave me peace.

"The relationship between me and my parents was getting ugly—it was bad. It was all because of what I was doing. I couldn't sleep. There was discomfort. My parents wanted me to go see a psychologist. They thought I was clinically depressed. I was losing hair, not eating properly. I was struggling."

She walked into practice one day sapped of energy—no joy, no smile, and no peace.

"All of that was stripped from me," she says. "I remember warming up for practice, and my coach was talking to me, but I really wasn't there. I got up on the beam, and I stood on the edge looking down. It's one of those moments that's really hard to explain. It's hard to understand."

That was the moment she heard the voice of God.

Shawn had grown up in a home that believed in God, but there wasn't a depth to that belief. "I knew there was a story that everybody taught," she says. "I knew there was a church, the idea of God. I just didn't feel like I knew him. My family would pray, but I lacked any real relationship with him. We weren't the every-Sunday churchgoing family, maybe Easter and Christmas."

But on that day as she stood on that beam, everything changed. "It was like in an instant, I felt the entire world just lifted off my shoulders. In that moment I felt God speak to me."

"You've been so distraught over this decision," she heard God say. "You've been putting yourself through all of this and your family through all of this. You've been afraid of disappointing a lot of people. Put it behind you."

"Perfectionism is like a drum," she says. "As a gymnast you're taught that nothing except perfection is acceptable. You're never thin enough. You're never good enough. You're never sticking your landings perfectly enough. But in that moment, I knew I could forever trust in God. I had taken myself so low that I needed Someone, some miracle to get me out of it. I felt euphoric. I drove myself home and cried my eyes out all the way home. I was just so at peace with everything. I heard God telling me it was all going to be okay."

Finally tasting the peace she'd thought only gold could give her, Shawn made the decision to retire. The sport she had trusted in so long for her identity, worth, and peace had finally proven unable to keep its promise.

"People say winning Olympic gold is the greatest success of your life," she says. "But when you stand up there on the podium, it's just a medal. I won the gold in balance beam. I distinctly remember winning and it not being the greatest thing in the world. I gave my heart and soul to get to that place, and it only validated that there would always be more. Gold is not the be-all end-all. It's not the answer to everything. But God is.

"The gift God has given me is peace. I can stop beating myself up. God gives and never expects anything in return. I could win twelve Olympic gold medals, and knowing God would still be my greatest reward, my proudest reward."

To find peace in your identity, you must give God control of your destiny. Peace comes when you trust his plan whether you succeed or fail; rise or fall; win gold, silver, or bronze; or even get disqualified. He is bigger than your weaknesses and loves you more than your failures.

It's a lesson Shawn Johnson learned in earning silver and a lesson that Albert Pujols learned in earning the Silver Slugger.

I CHOOSE PEACE

He reached the top of his sport, but came to understand that earning first in this world won't make you first in God's eyes. God's plan for life is not about what you earn but about what you give to others.

Chapter 8
Happy

the bigger game

ALBERT PUJOLS, MAJOR LEAGUE
BASEBALL ALL-STAR

People say the key to life is to do whatever makes you happy. But what if what you think will make you happy doesn't fully satisfy? Albert Pujols always knew that baseball was what he wanted to do with his life. It's what always made him happy. But he learned there is a bigger game than baseball. He would need something more than baseball stardom to win lasting happiness.

If you are at all into sports, you'll recognize the name Albert Pujols. But even if you don't know the name, his story can help point the way to true happiness—to finding the ease and peace, even joy, that some people seem to have. Things go wrong, things go right, and it doesn't seem to affect them. They seem touched by some magical fairy that keeps them smiling no matter what life throws at them. But there's nothing magical about that kind of peace and happiness. As Albert Pujols learned, it comes from learning what you really need and looking in the right place to find it.

From the time he was a boy, Albert's dream was always to be a baseball player. "That was life in the Dominican Republic. You go to school, you come back home, and you grab your baseball glove and bat. We'd play ball pretty much every day. But I never thought that later in my life I would have the opportunities that I did."

As of this writing, Albert Pujols's historic Major League Baseball career spans eighteen years and still counting. He's racked up ten all-star appearances, won six Silver Slugger Awards and two Gold Gloves. And he's one of only four players to reach both three thousand hits and six hundred home runs, a club that includes such greats as Willie Mays, Hank Aaron, and Alex Rodriguez. In 2009, *Sports Illustrated* even named him "Player of the Decade." But before all this, he was just a kid with a dream.

"Mom and Dad, they divorced when I was young in life," he says. "I was raised mostly by my grandma since I was three years old. We moved a lot. We stayed with members of my family, my aunts or my uncle. They got me a great education, supported me in everything that I did."

As with many in his native country, baseball ran in Albert's blood. Everybody around him played the game.

"My dad, my grandpa, my cousins, my whole family—everybody," he says. "It's in the blood of every Latin player. My dad would travel around the country as a softball pitcher. I wanted to be with him all the time and travel with him. He'd make sure I got a spot on the bus. Every time they had to travel,

I always had a spot to go with him. It's something that always sticks with you."

Pujols's family didn't always have much money. He remembers playing catch with limes and using a glove made from milk cartons. At times three generations and twelve members of his family had to share one house. They always had food, but sometimes it came via the local pawn shop.

"My family would take jewelry or other stuff to the pawn shop, and that's how we'd get two or three pounds of rice to feed the whole house. There were struggles. But we weren't poor like a lot of the people in the Dominican Republic. As a little boy you don't worry about the struggle. You're so young, all you care about is trying to grow up."

Albert dreamed of growing up and helping his family through his sport. "I remember telling my grandma that when I became this baseball player, I would buy her a big house anywhere she wanted. Those were the things I thought about. We had that struggle with money. But my family made it easy for me to just do my thing, go to school and play the game. My dad even figured out how to buy me a glove and bat."

One by one, as Albert was growing up, various family members would move to the United States. An aunt would move, then an uncle or a cousin and even his grandmother. Eventually, at age sixteen, Albert and his father joined them, settling in Independence, Missouri. But moving to a new country came with new challenges.

"I didn't know English at the time," he says, "so it was hard to go to school and finish my education. But my dad always told me to make sure that my education came first. That's something you can control. Baseball is like flipping a quarter. Heads you make it. Tails you don't. I always concentrated on the education."

Albert took near-daily English classes and picked up everything he could from his relatives who had moved there before him. Soon he had learned the language well enough to catch up to his peers at school.

"In life, you have to have those challenges," he says. "But I had support. Not everybody has that. My dad had to take a second job to make enough money for books so I could learn the language. It wasn't like a lot of students who would come here by themselves with no family. But it was still really hard. It was tough. I knew that if I wanted to succeed I had to go through the challenge."

Albert quickly found new outlets for his baseball passion, opportunities he didn't have in his home country. As a high schooler he won a spot in American Legion Baseball, an amateur league for kids his age, achieving an astonishing .593 batting average and thirty-five home runs. In his first year of community college his skill continued to shine, with a batting average of .461 and twenty-two home runs. At that point everyone knew he'd go pro. The only question was how early he would be selected in the draft. The earlier a team selects a player, the more they believe he will rise to the major leagues. It's a mark of confidence in a player's ability.

"I remember sitting on the couch with my girlfriend waiting for the call that would tell me I had been drafted by a pro team," Albert says. "There's nine o'clock, ten o'clock, one o'clock. I never got a call until almost two o'clock. I was really disappointed. I was expecting to go in the first couple of rounds. Instead, I got picked 402nd in the draft."

Albert had met his girlfriend, Deidre—later to be his wife—while in high school. Neither spoke the other's language well, but they quickly fell in love anyway. They exchanged phone numbers, and Deidre made the first move.

"She called me every day for a whole week. She wanted to set up a day for us to go out, but I was either at school or work. My grandma never gave me the message. Finally I came home from a baseball game and the phone rang."

On their first date, Deidre explained that she had a daughter from a previous relationship. Isabella was just three months old and had Down syndrome. The genetic disorder comes with physical growth delays, speech problems, and cognitive disabilities. There is no cure, and those who have it require a lifetime of additional parental support.

"I didn't even know what Down syndrome was," Albert remembers. "Deidre was trying to find out how to tell me in Spanish because my English wasn't that good. But as soon as she introduced me to Isabella, I knew from that moment that Deidre and I were going to get married." (They would marry that year, and eventually a son named AJ would join their family.)

And it was Deidre who sat next to Albert as he waited for his call into professional baseball. When the phone finally rang in the thirteenth round with word that he'd been drafted by the St. Louis Cardinals, he nearly quit. He had hoped to get drafted in the first two rounds. But pro teams worried about his swing, his large body size, and how he'd fit into a defensive position. College success does not always translate to professional ball. Tampa Bay had that year's number-one pick. They had expressed early interest in Albert, even calling him for a predraft workout and scouting session. But he'd failed to convince the team's scouting director.

"All that hard work I'd put into it," he says. "And here I am at 402 in the draft. I almost quit. I even told Deidre that if I didn't make it to the majors within two years, I'd quit baseball."

Baseball has a tiered system of professional baseball leagues. Drafted players go first to a series of minor league teams until finally rising to Major League Baseball if they can prove themselves capable. Most players never even make it out of the minor leagues, especially lower drafts like Pujols. But he was determined to get to the majors no matter what. "Getting drafted at 402 made me want to prove those people wrong," he admits. "I had a chip on my shoulder."

Early in their relationship, Deidre had told him she went to church and needed him to go too. He'd grown up Catholic, but, like many in his family, he was Catholic in name only. He attended church occasionally, but nobody in his family went regularly.

"I knew there was a God," Pujols says. "But I didn't have the faith. I didn't have that belief. Nobody in my house was raised in church. I never saw that. To me what was natural was to go to school, play baseball, and have friends."

Nevertheless, he followed Deidre to church and began to see that he'd missed something. He saw that faith was more than just a cultural label or a religious tag. He wanted the new life he heard the church people talking about.

"I wasn't a crazy party guy," he says. "I would go out a lot and never drink, never smoke. That wasn't something that attracted me. But I started going through the Bible, going to church, and I would walk out of there with different information. I wanted what other people had at church—that joy, that passion, and that love. I wanted that. I felt that I had an empty hole inside that I needed to fill. I wanted to change my life."

Every week the church service would end with a call to come forward and make a decision to follow Jesus. Albert had never even seen something like this in church before. They called it an invitation.

"What is this?" he asked Deidre. She explained it, and the next week he went up.

"They took me through the Scriptures," he says. "I dedicated my life to the Lord. I surrendered myself and told God to take control of my life. My whole life I had tried to do it by myself, and that didn't work."

Up to this point, Albert's life had always been about baseball, school, or friends. But giving his life to God set a new direction and a new priority in his life.

"I made that decision, and my life began changing," he says. "It's transforming, like 360 degrees. I was concentrating more on what God wanted me to do and not the things that I wanted to do myself."

This change spread to the rest of his life as well. He quickly found success in the minor leagues, putting up a .314 batting average and nineteen home runs. That won him a spot on the St. Louis Cardinals lineup the following year in the major leagues.

"Everything started changing," he says. "Success came. Everything just came so quick."

Albert Pujols received the honor of Rookie of the Year and then was named an MLB all-star, an award he'd win every year but one for the next decade. Proving every skeptic wrong, Pujols shot from no-name draft pick to the league's most sought-after young talent.

"Every day there's people coming to me, telling me how great a baseball player I am," he says. "I'll have some parents say to me that I'm their little boy's hero. But I tell them that I'm just a baseball player. God is our hero, who died on the cross for our sins. That's who your little boy needs to follow and keep his eyes on.

"I love being a baseball player, believe me. But I don't want people to remember me as a great baseball player, I want people to remember me as a loving daddy who loves the Lord, a godly husband, and an example for my kids. That's the more important thing. Baseball is great, but off the field is more important than what I do on the field.

"It's not about me. It's about God—serving him, his will and his work. If you asked me twenty years ago, I would have told you that I thought it was about me. But I found somebody to fill that hole that I had in me, and that was Jesus Christ, when he died on the cross for my sins."

Jesus once said that "many who are first will be last, and many who are last will be first."[1] We won't argue who's the "first" or greatest in baseball, but Albert Pujols is at least an honorable mention in the debate. Despite his legendary career, however, baseball is not where Pujols puts his hope in life. It's not where he gets ultimate meaning or lasting happiness. Plenty of great athletes enjoy their sport but fail to achieve peace in their hearts. Albert Pujols found peace not because he played great ball, but because he knew there is a bigger game to play.

Standout MLB pitcher R. A. Dickey faced this same realization while chasing his baseball dream. But he carried with him a childhood trauma that brought him to the brink of suicide. He tried to cover up the pain with sports achievement. But no matter how thickly he painted over it, insecurity still bled through. It was only at the brink of death that he finally found the peace he needed.

Chapter 9
Shame

I felt less than human

R. A. DICKEY, MAJOR LEAGUE BASEBALL
PITCHER AND CY YOUNG AWARD WINNER

What would it be like to swim across the Missouri River? R. A. Dickey thought as he stood on the river's banks in Omaha, Nebraska. *How legendary would it be to do that in front of my teammates?*

He'd need to cross nearly seven hundred feet of the world's fourth-longest river. The Missouri drains more than five hundred thousand square miles of land and gathers its silty contents to stretch over some twenty-three hundred miles. It's a pretty spectacular river, and swimming across it would be legendary indeed.

That would go down in history, he thought.

R. A. Dickey had something to prove. He'd already spent

years bouncing in and out of baseball's major leagues—good enough to make it in but not good enough to stay. He was a power pitcher on the tail end of a long but disappointing professional career. His pitches were falling in speed, dropping from the low nineties to the high eighties, squarely in the realm of mediocrity. His arm took longer and longer to recover after each game. He now stood on the banks of the Missouri, knowing that if he had to prove himself, it wouldn't be with a baseball. Maybe a river would do?

"I was really searching for some validation," R. A. says. "If I'm not going to be a good baseball player, at least I can validate myself by taking this risk and achieving this thing."

Word spread among the team that R. A. was going to swim across the Missouri. The team's hotel sat right on the bank of the river. Teammates gathered at the shore and peered from their room windows.

They're going to tell this story forever, R. A. thought.

He stripped down and dove into the water to the cheers and guffaws of his teammates. He put his head down and started to stroke toward the opposite shore. After swimming awhile he decided to pull up and check his progress.

"I was about a quarter of the way out," he says. "I couldn't see anybody. The current was so fast that it had taken me several hundred yards downriver."

Even as R. A. treaded water, he found himself sliding farther downstream. The river's undertow pulled at his legs, sucking him down and forcing ever more exertion to stay afloat. But he decided to keep going. He stretched out and continued across the river, head down and arms stroking one after the other.

"I'm starting to get really fatigued," he remembers. "I poke up again to see where I am, and I'm almost to the halfway point. I think to myself there is no way I can get to the other side."

Panic set in. He wasn't even halfway across and was already struggling to keep his head above water.

"It was either keep pressing on and die trying or swallow my pride and try and make it back to shore and survive," he says. "After treading water for a few seconds, I decided to go back to the bank that I started from . . . if I could."

But it quickly became apparent that even this goal might be impossible to achieve. Less than one hundred feet from the shore, he started to sink.

"I didn't have anything left," he remembers. "My muscles were burning. The lactic acid was building up in my joints. I could hardly lift my arm to stroke."

He would take a stroke and then bob under the water. He'd force himself back to the surface, take another stroke, and then dip back under. "I'd try to swim underwater for a few seconds and then come to the top. But I couldn't continue to do even that. So I finally surrendered to the river. That was it. I was going to die."

Regret and memories filled his mind. Thoughts of his wife and three kids overwhelmed him.

"I remember being so repentant underwater. I was saying sorry to God for leaving my family. I'm leaving my kids without a father. I was actually weeping underwater. I was coming to the end."

Much had happened to bring him to this moment. A man

who needs to prove himself is a man carrying a weight. And in this case, the weight was shame that began in his childhood after a series of confusing and painful events.

"The first time that it happened was with a female babysitter," he says. "I was eight years old, and she was twelve or thirteen. She was the person given the responsibility of being my caregiver. I was put in a position where that wasn't the case."

R. A. recalled a childhood memory that he had buried deep. He had never even spoken of it until well into adulthood.

"Nobody was there except me and her. The next thing I knew, I'm in the dark, sweating. Clothes are off. I don't know why. I don't know what's going on."

Confusion was the overriding emotion. R. A. was too young to understand and too shamed to ask or even to tell.

"I felt so wicked and afraid," he says. "A lot of fear and sadness. But the sadness didn't come until later. In the moment, I'm just completely overwhelmed with confusion and loneliness.

"I have often asked myself why I didn't run or fight. The answer is fear. I felt paralyzed. I've felt a lot of shame for not running and not fighting. But in the moment, you don't really know what's going on. What starts as a game turns into a nightmare, and it's over so quickly."

The most vivid memory is the way it smelled—the smell of the room and the smell of the dark, of being under the covers.

"That's what I remember the most," he says. "That's what makes it the most real for me, the way it smelled. It just smelled like something was happening that shouldn't be happening. It forever stained my mind, that smell. There were about a half a dozen incidents over that summer with that babysitter. When I got to the place where I knew it was inevitable, I just wanted it to be over. I would block myself off to it. It would be like an out-of-body experience. I would remove myself."

But later that summer, something even more traumatic happened.

"It was more aggressive," he says. "It was violent."

R. A. had gone with his mother and sister to visit relatives in the country. He was playing by himself with a tennis ball, bouncing it off the roof, when he suddenly noticed an older boy standing behind him.

"The thing I remember most about the incident was that I knew it was coming," he says. "I knew I was about to be overtaken, to be raped. I tried to play dead. It was over so quickly. I went somewhere else in my mind. Then I came back, and I got up and was bleeding."

The loneliness, fear, and confusion stung as before. What had happened? *Why* had it happened?

"I remember the ride home afterward. I tried to count the dashed line in the middle of the street all the way home so I wouldn't have to think about what had just happened. I considered telling someone but was unwilling to risk it. I thought I had played a part in it. I did not want the judgment. I did not want anybody to know how wicked I felt or how damaged.

"The first attribute that I developed after the abuse was the ability to escape. I became an escape artist, not wanting to risk anything below the surface with anyone. I could convince you that I was someone that I really wasn't. It was a way to protect myself."

This trait would follow R. A. throughout his life. He could smile while crying on the inside. The jolly, happy version of himself masked the fear on the inside. He doubted that anyone could love him if they found out the truth of his past.

"I felt like if I were to tell somebody they would want nothing to do with me. So I kept it closed, never uttered a word of it until I was thirty-two years old. One of the things that happens when you're abused is you feel less than human. Do I even matter? Why should I be here? If that can happen to me, then I must be less than an ant. You don't have anywhere to go with it.

"In my darkest moment, I was sitting in a driveway with a rubber hose duct-taped to the exhaust pipe, the windows rolled up, a towel packed around the slit, and my hand on the key. That's how dark it was for me. I felt so much shame from a broken past."

Long before that, however, he found another kind of escape in sports. "I got lost in being a basketball player, a baseball player, a football player," he says. "It was a way for me to have some identity outside of being a victim of sexual abuse. If you were close to me at the time, you would never have guessed what had happened."

In sports R. A. learned that if he worked hard enough, if he executed just the right mechanism, he could control his own fate. He could be the master and not the victim. "If you followed the formula as an athlete, then you would be rewarded for that," R. A. says. "That was not true outside of the athletic culture."

R. A. quarterbacked his high school football team, but gradually focused on baseball as his sport of choice. He went on to be a star pitcher for the University of Tennessee Volunteers, only to be drafted out of college by the Texas Rangers and offered a contract to play ball. He flew to Arlington, Texas, to meet team officials and sign the contract. "I had dreamed about pitching in the big leagues since I was eight years old," he says. "My dreams were finally going to be realized."

R. A. traveled down with his agent to sign, but he needed to pass a physical examination first. They ran him through a battery of tests, including one that assessed a key ligament in the elbow called the ulnar collateral ligament. A common injury among pitchers is the weakening or tearing of this ligament, which causes an instability in the joint and reduces range of motion. They took an X-ray and found a millimeter of extra laxity in R. A.'s elbow, a sign that the ligament might be compromised.

"I didn't think anything of it," he says. "I've thrown a thousand pitches, a million pitches. I was sure there was some wear and tear in there, but it shouldn't have been any more than anybody else who had been drafted."

They left the doctor's office and headed to the stadium with the results.

"They called my agent into the office and asked me to wait outside," he says. "That didn't feel right to me. Something felt out of place."

His agent came out minutes later, his eyes watery. They called R. A. into the office.

"They wanted me to get a second opinion," he says. "They wouldn't give me a contract until I did. It was all I could do in the moment not to reach over the desk and pummel him with all my might."

R. A. headed to Alabama to meet with an orthopedic specialist. He ran more tests. Everything showed up clear.

"I don't think there's anything wrong with you," the doctor said. "But we've got to take an MRI."

They injected his elbow with dye and ran him through the MRI machine. What they found shocked not just R. A. but his doctor as well.

"I've never seen anything like this," the doctor said. "You don't have an ulnar collateral ligament at all in your right elbow. I don't know what to tell you. You just don't have one."

"I had this feeling of inadequacy," R. A. says. "I was damaged goods. It opened up all kinds of wounds. I'd been trying to put gauze pads on top of my past. I had controlled what I could. I had been drafted as a first-round draft pick, but it still wasn't enough."

The Rangers took a risk on R. A. Dickey and gave him a contract offer despite the test results, but with a severe cut in pay and a lot of doubt in his future. They stuck him in the bottom of the minor leagues.

"I felt behind the eight ball from the beginning," he remembers. "I was the freak that didn't have a ligament. I felt I had to do everything better and more perfectly than the guy to my left or right. That's what it would take to get to the next level."

But no matter how hard he tried, R. A.'s past kept crawling back into the present.

"I fought a lot with my wife," he remembers. "I didn't get paid enough to support my family in the minor leagues. That caused fights. The feeling of inadequacy kept coming back. I would have a good outing in a game, and I'd feel good. Then after a bad outing, I would be upset and distant. I wasn't navigating life very well. My marriage was in trouble."

He spent the next several years in and out of the major leagues. Then his pitching started showing signs of age. His speed dropped, and he knew his career would soon hit a cold end.

"I could see the writing on the wall," he says. "I was self-aware enough to know that if I didn't come up with something else, my career was over." So he decided to take some advice he'd been given and work at becoming a full-time knuckleball pitcher.

One of the rarest pitches in baseball, and certainly the strangest, the knuckleball produces a pitch with no spin on the ball. The lack of spin creates erratic movement in the pitch. The movement can be so unpredictable that some catchers have had to use specialized gloves just to catch the ball. The trick, of course, is creating erratic movement that still gets over the strike zone. The advantage for pitchers like R. A. is that knuckleballs don't require the speed that other pitches do. If mastered, the pitch could give R. A. years more in the sport.

R. A. Dickey dropped down to the minor leagues to perfect his new weapon in the hopes of extending his career. He found early success and got a shot again in the majors. But in his first major-league outing, he tied a record for the most home runs given up in a game—a statistic no pitcher wants to see on his résumé.

"I was promptly sent down to the minors the next day and taken off the roster. My hopes were dashed against the rocks. I was at the precipice again. All the shame and inadequacy. I'd had so much hope tied up in being this knuckleballer."

For years R. A. had buried his past, his shame, and his hurt in layer after layer of sports-related achievements, or at least the dream of achievements. If baseball ended, so would his escape. If his career stopped here, he'd have to face what he'd never had the strength to face before. That's when he decided to swim across the Missouri River. Maybe this way he could finally prove himself unbroken, undamaged, and worthy. Maybe this way he could find peace from the pain of the past.

But it wasn't to be. He had failed to cross the river and now struggled even to make it back to shore.

"I was coming to the end," he remembers. "I prayed that God would not make it painful. I continued to sink. I was weeping. I decided to open my mouth and take in the water so that it would end more quickly."

But in the split second before he did so, his feet hit solid ground. He had sunk to the bottom of the river. "I wasn't sure how deep it was," he says. "But I felt like I could push off the bottom and maybe with a stroke or two I could make my way up."

He pushed himself to the surface and took another breath. He sank again to the bottom and pushed off again. He repeated this, and each time he reached the top he'd take a gasp of air before sinking again.

"I felt an adrenaline surge," he says. "I was able to pump out a couple more strokes until I could see the riverbank and a place where I might get to."

One teammate, Grant Balfour, had run along the shore, following R. A. all the way. "I got about ten yards from the bank, and he was up ahead of me," R. A. says. "He had his hand out. It was enough to motivate me for a couple more strokes. I reached out and grabbed his hand, and he pulled me to shore. I survived when I had totally surrendered myself to the end. God had preserved my life for whatever was coming next. I didn't know what that was. Things changed for me after this."

Coming within a breath of dying woke R. A. Dickey to greater truths. He realized that he had nothing to prove. He had let his past pain bring him to the point of drowning in the Missouri River. But he was more than his pain, more than his past abuse. And he was more than an athlete. Life was bigger. His identity was bigger. He had to make changes.

"Baseball shifted into the proper perspective," he says. "As long as I hung on so tightly to my career and my identity as an athlete, God was just cranking my finger back so that he could get at what he wanted. I resolved to let my career be what it was going to be."

R. A. stopped obsessing over what might happen in his career. He stopped worrying if it might end and just worried about the moment, the present. His pitching steadily improved from there.

"I didn't have an expectation anymore," he says. "That freed me up to be better. My only expectation was that I was going to come to the field and commit to my craft in a moment-by-moment scenario. I didn't need to worry about my last pitch or my next pitch, just the moment that I was in."

In 2012 Dickey was named to the National League all-star team for the first time in his career. The year ended with him winning the Cy Young Award, the only knuckleballer in MLB history to ever win the game's highest pitching award. And his on-the-field accolades paired with his off-the-field successes.

"I surrendered to the process of unpacking my past with a therapist," he says. "I was starting to get pieces of myself back. I was encouraged. It was the beginning of a journey. I talked for the first time about my abuse."

Talking to a professional about his past proved a big step in the healing process, but he still had never shared his past with his wife. This, he found, had poisoned his ability to truly engage in the relationship. He'd kept his true self away from her, hidden who he was for fear she'd reject him. Now he invited her to a therapy session, where he planned to tell her the truth of his past. Even then, he didn't fully trust her. He didn't believe she would still love him or see him as anything but inadequate and damaged.

"I was totally ready for her to walk out," he says. "That's what I felt like I deserved. I was prepared for her to end the marriage. I came completely clean to her about being sexually abused. Any lies that I had told her or truths I'd kept from her, I laid it all out there. I let God be in control of it."

There's a metaphor for this in the knuckleball. The pitcher can't know where the ball is going to cross the plate. That's the point of the pitch; it's unpredictable. Its exact course is hidden to the batter, catcher, and pitcher. You just throw the ball with all the skill and determination you can and trust it'll go where you need it to go.

"You have to surrender to the outcome with this pitch in a way that you don't with other pitches," he says. "Surrendering to God is like that. You take life moment by moment and trust him for the end. I have a responsibility to use the equipment that I've been given, to wake up in the morning and surrender every moment until I close my eyes again at night, but he's in charge of the results."

R. A. decided to tell his wife everything. He spilled out his pain and his past, his struggle to trust anyone, including her. He had never truly let himself be known. He did so now, fearing it would cost him the very relationship he was hoping to save. But he did it knowing the risk was worth the chance to love and be loved for who he really was and not some fake version of himself.

"She did the opposite of what I thought she'd do," he says. "She completely embraced me. Despite what I thought were the ugliest things about me and about my past, she loved me. That did so much for the way that I began to trust human beings again. It let me take risks in relationships, risk trusting people, trusting other men, which I had never been able to do because of my past wounds."

For the first time in his life, R. A. realized someone loved the real him, past and all. He didn't have to hide. His wife's love didn't see damaged goods when she looked at him, just a man whom she loved. And her acceptance helped him believe that who he was amounted to more than what he achieved in baseball or what others had done to him. R. A. Dickey was R. A. Dickey, no matter what had happened in the past or would happen in the future.

"I can be redeemed from sexual abuse," he says. "I am not

that. That's a part of my story, but it does not define me. To be redeemed out of that mentality—that's powerful. Jesus wants to take your story and make it different. He wants to redeem it. I discovered there was a freedom in that. I didn't have to hide anymore."

In 2018, after more than twenty years in professional baseball, R. A. Dickey announced his retirement, but in a sense his life story is just beginning. He has discovered a peace and stillness in redefining his life's aim to be about relationship instead of achievement. Baseball is something he did, but not who he was. Sexual abuse is something that happened to him, but it's not him. He found peace by risking love and making his life about that love, not about his past or his career.

"When I took the risk of trusting another human being, I found that there was a lot of redemption in that," he says. "I've come to the place in my life where I believe that's why I'm on earth; it's to do relationship well. In those relationships I see a tangible Jesus, and that does much for my spirit."

Jesus said something like this when he said, "Love the Lord your God . . . and love your neighbor as yourself. All the Law and Prophets hang on these two commands." Love and relationship sit at the core of what it means to be human. They are life's true purpose and primary reasons for being.

Sometimes we make Jesus too complicated. There is a lot of confusing stuff in the Bible, things we can argue about. But love—this idea of relationship that R. A. is talking about—is the point of it all. It's why we are all here.

Peace, freedom—that breath of fresh air and clarity in life

comes only when you spend your life seeking and giving that which you were designed to seek and give. When you see beyond achievement and labels, you can get a sense of that true purpose in life. Whether you're a citizen or foreigner, whether you're black, white, or brown, whether you flip burgers or flip houses, none of that matters in defining who you are and your value. Love is free of all that. Love just says, "I matter, and so do you." Hip-hop artist Propaganda struggled with this concept growing up in an ethnically divided and violent neighborhood. He battled to know that his color or economic situation didn't change his status as equally human and, therefore, as equally valuable.

Chapter 10
Race

why I matter

JASON "PROPAGANDA" PETTY, HIP-HOP ARTIST, ACTIVIST

I was born the wrong color, in the wrong neighborhood," says hip-hop artist and YouTube phenomenon Jason "Propaganda" Petty. He grew up in a Hispanic neighborhood in south-central Los Angeles—a black kid who spoke Spanish.

"My father was a Black Panther from back in the civil rights days," he says. "He grew up hard and struggled. He taught me black is beautiful. I thought everybody thought that. He was super militant about it, but I was the only black kid anyone in my neighborhood knew. I got teased because of my color. My identity was forged in this crucible of a real culture clash."

Jason faced more than just a clash of colors in a neighborhood marked by violence and poverty. But as he explains it, "I was super oblivious. I didn't even know it was as dangerous as it was. I just thought that's how people live. You can call it sheltered.

I CHOOSE PEACE

My parents wanted to get us out of the projects but couldn't. It was a war zone. We were all just trying to survive, just trying to live.

"I can remember getting chased, just trying to walk home. I didn't see it as unusual at the time. It's looking back, little things I picked up on later. Like my neighbor's house got set on fire twice, once by the dad. He burned the house down. They moved out, and it turned into a crack house. I didn't know it then; I just thought they didn't turn on their electricity. I thought it was like camping—maybe they were cooking with candles, you know? I was just oblivious."

Jason never joined a gang. His father and the men in his life made sure of that. They also made sure he knew that school was not optional for him. "You go to school, you finish a degree, you keep going—that's what my father taught me. He went to UCLA, got his degree. He taught me to be a better image of what the black man is. Let the world see it."

But in order to survive, Jason also learned the rules of living in the neighborhood and spoke the language. And he continued to struggle with the pressures surrounding him.

When he'd get chased walking home, the men at his church challenged him to take it as a test of his character. "Be a man," they'd say. "You going to let them change the way you walk home? Stand up. Don't fall victim."

"These men taught me that these other dudes are followers," he says. "How much more bravery does it take to not join this gang, to not sell drugs in this kind of environment."

Along the way, Jason learned that his environment affects

him but doesn't make him. What surrounded him revealed his identity but didn't need to alter that identity. You can live next to a crack house and not do crack. You can live amidst gangs, violence, and racial tensions and come out clean.

"I learned there's a purpose for my life," he says. "I'm not going to be what you say you want me to be. You're not going to change it."

Discovering your purpose and your identity doesn't happen in a flash or in a night. It takes time. It takes the trials of life. Hardship tests a person's core. Truth comes out in the fire.

"I like to say that I was slow-cooked. I would say it started in sixth grade and then culminated at age sixteen. Examining my experience in life and just always feeling like I don't belong. I was born the wrong color, in the wrong neighborhood, in the wrong decade, to the wrong parents."

But it was just this mismatched upbringing that gave Jason his voice and perspective. He lived within the culture of gangs, violence, and racial tension but never fully belonged to it. His time in church showed him a path beyond it.

"My pastor was brilliant," he says. "He talked over my head, but he was brilliant. Mostly, I just remember hearing that he took the Scriptures very serious. You understood, listening to him, that this is the Word of God. This is what God gave us to explain himself to us. I don't know if I really understood anything else he said, but what stuck with me is that we ain't playing around with the Word of God. This is serious."

With that in his head, his father gave him some verses from the Psalms:

> You created my inmost being;
>
> > You knit me together in my mother's womb.
>
> I praise you because I am fearfully and wonderfully made;
>
> > Your works are wonderful,
> >
> > > I know that full well.[1]

When he heard this, Jason knew God was an Artist with a purpose. The color of his skin, the sound of his voice, the neighborhood that shaped him—none of this was a mistake. God had painted every stroke of his life into existence, color included. And he did it on purpose because color matters.

"The colors are not wrong," he says. "They're powerful brushstrokes. A lot of things came into perspective. Growing up, dudes on the street used to call me yanta. I didn't know what it meant till later, but it's a dis, a racial slur. But now I hear something new: 'You are fearfully and wonderfully made. This ain't a mistake. You're exactly what I want you to be.'"

Jason found a home in hip-hop, a place where the artist in him could shine. He dove into it and started competing in weekly rap battles, a freestyle impromptu form of rap in which two artists attempt to outwit, out-rhyme, and out-rap the other.

"I'd thrown myself into this hip-hop culture," he says, "because I thought maybe over here somebody would like me. I didn't fit anywhere else. Maybe my life would have purpose in this."

He won rap battles and developed a name for himself. But that passage in Psalm 139 that his father had given him inspired him to something more.

"This verse let me see something," he says. "I don't have personhood because I can freestyle better than this other dude. That verse finally made me realize that God had a purpose for me. Every hurt, every failure, every miserable despicable moment I had to endure, being spit on walking home. Now I hear I'm fearfully and wonderfully made. This junk was on purpose."

"I'm a graffiti artist too," he says. "And I know it's the same. A lot of times I'm laying down colors that won't be seen at the end. But I know they need to be there because I'm the artist. How crazy would it be for the picture itself to tell me that I don't know what I'm doing? I'm drawing a face, then the face says, 'You're drawing me wrong.' Who are you to tell the artist that he's not drawing you right?"

Jason has known the power of pain to make one stronger. "I think of my auntie," he says in his song "Beautiful Pain." "She ain't embarrassed of her scars. It proves that she's cancerless. Breastless, not breathless." And in the same song he describes himself as "a last-born rightful heir to the throne, son of a nobody with poverty in my bones, and that's beautiful."

Beauty often rises from pain. Something sure can come from the trials and hardships of life. You'd never choose the challenges on your own. But when hard times are thrown your way and you overcome them, you find a strength and a truth about who God made you to be.

Jason discovered his identity etched in the fire. He found the truth of who he was by finding who he was in the hard times. He can face future pain with strength and sureness because he knows that God carved a truth and a strength into his soul, and he has the scars to prove it. God knows his pain, knows his color, and knows he matters.

It's a lesson a remarkable woman named Jonita had to learn as well. Jonita wears a deep ebony skin and a broad white smile carried on the muscled physique of a college tennis star. Jonita grew up African American in the deep South, where racial prejudice lived and breathed unfiltered.

"In college," Jonita says, "I often found myself the only black person in a crowd. There were many bumps in the road and times of frustration or loneliness from being misunderstood. The first time I ever heard the term *color-blind* was while attending a predominately white church. But when I looked in the mirror, I didn't see a translucent face staring back. I wondered why that part of me was not worth seeing or acknowledging."

Jonita decided to address the racial divide she found in her community. She started with her church.

"My husband and I joined a small group in our church. We would meet weekly, share a meal, and share life. We were the only black family in this group, but it didn't matter. We felt connected and loved. Then Ferguson happened."

In August 2014, Michael Brown Jr., a young African American man, was fatally shot by a white police officer in the city of Ferguson, Missouri. The killing brought issues of police brutality, racial profiling, and racial bias to the national consciousness. Riots and protests erupted the day after the shooting, but months later a grand jury declined to indict the officer involved.

For many, the event meant nothing more than a chance to discuss some abstract legal case that happened in some Midwestern town. But for people of color, people like Jonita, it was personal. Racism wasn't an abstract construct. It wasn't a theory. She was surrounded by its effects. She lived daily in its quiet cruelty.

"The image of Michael Brown being shot and the turmoil, division, and anger that swept the nation left me reeling," she says. "Even today I tell my husband not to go out in his hoodie at night. I thought surely the people in my group would offer some type of solace on the Sunday after—a prayer, hope for healing. No need to take sides on who did what, but a vocal standing together."

But her church and her group remained silent. The week passed as if nothing had happened.

"I have often realized that being the only black person in the room means I'll be surrounded by ignorance of what I am faced with," she says. "I see the systemic racism and individual racism in the world. It's real and prevalent. But I also see the good news of Jesus as being bigger than the broken systems of the world. The goal has to be bigger than overcoming racism—to live a life loving, serving, and learning from those who are like us but different. I am not only my blackness. It's nothing that needs to be shunned, discriminated against, or ignored. Jesus redeemed us from this kind of discrimination. He came to bring us together."

Jonita clings to this hope despite the tears she shed in realizing not everyone in her church community would hear or understand her plight. It's a hope and a trust that the great Artist knows what he's doing, that he's creating a masterpiece in her. She's beautiful, even if others struggle to see or prize it.

I CHOOSE PEACE

Whether it's the color of your skin, the size of your waist, or the shape of your face, God made you beautiful. You are his masterpiece. You are that before you are anything else. No other name and no other label can undo this reality.

Finding Peace in **Difficulty** and **Disappointment**

Hope names the darkness. It's not a blind optimism or a naïve dream. Hope sees the squalor and the filth. It cries at the pain and shouts at the injustice. Hope doesn't deny the unpleasant realities of this life. It sees past them.

Hope admits both the brokenness of this world and the power of God to fix it. Hope is a faith in better times to come and a better place to belong. It doesn't claim to have everything figured out but believes in the One who does. It doesn't pretend perfection but believes in the Perfecter.

In this final part of the book you'll find stories of people who have found peace in difficulty and disappointment. They were tempted by this disappointment. They felt a pull toward despair. But they chose instead to hope and in hoping they found peace.

They don't have clean and easy tales. You won't envy their journey, but you'll want the lessons they picked up along the way. They speak of pain and loss. They've been addicted, sick, broken, and abandoned. But they've also tasted healing, even though they may not have its fullness yet. Their struggles continue; their stories point to hope and, ultimately, to peace.

Chapter 11
Trapped

when Jesus makes it worse

BRIAN "HEAD" WELCH, KORN LEAD GUITARIST

I loved partying," Brian Welch says, recalling years touring as the lead guitarist for the heavy-metal band Korn.

"I loved money. I worshiped money. I had been brought up where money was important. Where I came from, you needed money to be respected. If you set yourself up right, then you were all good. I had a mentality where I had to get a certain amount of money so I wouldn't have to worry. Money was my thing."

But money wasn't enough. Korn's debut album broke into the Billboard Top 100; later albums rose even higher. They headlined giant worldwide tours and sold millions of records. The money flowed in. And Brian, whose stage name was Head, loved performing. The music blaring. The lights and the volume filling his senses. The crowd screaming for more. The show filled his veins with adrenaline. His long, braided hair swayed with the thump of the drums and the screaming of guitars.

"There was a high when I went onstage and saw all these people loving my music and loving me. There were all these girls after me and people worshiping and going nuts for me. I was puffed up on the inside. I started thinking, *I'm important.*"

But it wasn't enough. The shows would end, and an emptiness would linger despite the band's success. The party after the show grew in an attempt to fill it. That's when the drugs crept in—especially cocaine and methamphetamine.

"I couldn't let the night end," he says. "I couldn't bear the silence. Onstage I was on this high and I did not want to come down."

The drugs helped him hold on to that feeling. They brought relief from the emptiness, but the relief never lasted. The happiness never stayed.

Then Brian's daughter, Jennea, came into the world. And Brian was sure everything was going to be different.

"It was a such a euphoric feeling," he remembers. "Jennea was beautiful. I loved her. I thought my life could feel that way forever. The whole thing just felt spiritual. I thought I was going to be happy forever."

But Brian still loved performing—and partying. He had given up drugs when Jennea was born, but gradually drugs and alcohol crept back into his life. It all began wearing on this family and on his relationships, especially because his wife was using too.

Then one day she called to say she was leaving. "I don't want to have anything to do with you. I don't want to talk with you.

And I'm leaving Jennea with you. I got a babysitter who will watch her for you."

"I became a single father right then," Brian says. And from that point on, Brian took over Jennea's care. He even brought her along on his tours.

"But I couldn't stay sober," he says. "I didn't know how."

"I had sworn that I would never do methamphetamine again," he says. "I saw what it did to my child's mother. It just took her feelings away and made her leave her own child. I just wanted my wife dead. I wanted to kill her for what she did. I thought my wife was the scum of the earth. How could she do drugs and let the drugs win her like that? But I ended up with an everyday crippling addiction to methamphetamine, and everything that I said about my ex-wife came true for me."

One evening before a show, Brian looked at Jennea, who by then was six years old. She was singing. Her little voice was beautiful.

"Wait? What are you singing?" Brian could not believe it. His daughter was singing one of his own songs. She was singing "A.D.I.D.A.S.," with its repetitive chorus of "All day I dream about sex."

The full weight of his crumbling life fell on him. "What am I doing? I'm a junkie, my daughter is singing 'All day I dream about sex,' and I'm going to die."

Shaken, he met with a friend named Eric, who shared with him—of all things—a scripture.

"I don't mean to be weird with you," Eric said with shyness written in his eyes. "I hope you don't take this the wrong way.

I've never done this before, so I don't really know how to do this, but I felt like this would mean something to you. It's Matthew 11:28: 'Come to me, all you who are weary and burdened, and I will give you rest.'"

The Bible verse struck a powerful chord in Brian's soul. He had tried everything he knew to get pleasure out of this life, but he had come up empty. He'd reached for the stars and seen his wildest dreams come true. He'd made more money and gotten more fame than he ever thought would come from playing a guitar. But his burden had never left. The hole in his heart had never filled. And now his life was spiraling out of control.

He wanted peace. He wanted rest. But he couldn't find it. He'd thought the path to happiness was pleasure, wealth, or success. Then when his daughter was born, he'd thought maybe satisfaction lay in being a father, but that, too, had failed him.

"I'm weary and burdened, and I do need rest for my soul," he said to himself. He felt the verse cry into his soul.

Eric and his wife invited Brian to church a couple of weeks later. He heard the verse again there. The pastor actually spoke about it. Brian felt God calling him, and he found himself answering.

"Jesus, you got to take these drugs from me," he said in one last desperate prayer. "Search me right now. Search my heart. You know I want to stop. Take them away. I can't do it on my own.

"Suddenly it felt like heaven invaded earth all around me, and I was just in awe of the feeling of ecstatic bliss. I looked up, and I was shaking."

In that moment Brian felt God. He couldn't explain it. He

couldn't define it. But he knew God was there. He knew God had heard his prayer.

"My heart was so changed that I said to my daughter, 'Jennea, Daddy's going to be home with you all the time. I'm quitting my career.' And her face lit up; she felt so special."

When the I Am Second team first met Brian, his story ended there. He'd quit the band, given up drugs, and dedicated his life to Jesus and his daughter. His decision rocked the band, his followers, and the world of music. We helped him share his story just as I Am Second launched. His film became the most viewed and talked-about story on our site. It was an epic tale of a rock star coming to Jesus: a god of the music world finds Jesus and walks away from it all to find peace. But what neither of us knew then was that Brian's life was about to get far worse before it ever got better.

"Never in Jennea's whole life did she have a parent home," Brian says, "one that wasn't going to leave." He wanted to be that father. And he honestly thought that with Jesus everything would change. His craving for drugs had gone away instantly, and he assumed the rest of the journey would be as simple. Suddenly he'd be a great father, a savvy businessman, and a spokesman for the faith.

"I moved to Phoenix just to get away from everything," he says. "I wanted to start over. I wanted Jesus to be my role model. I had a few million dollars in the bank. I was off on a mission to help the world and to use that money to change the world."

But doing the right thing is rarely easy. God doesn't paint a yellow-brick road for us to follow in life. Most steps are lit up one at a time or only in hindsight. And most people make plenty of missteps along the way.

That was certainly true of Brian. "I was following God," he remembers. "I wanted to go where I needed to be to get to my destiny with God. But I immediately started making bad choices after I quit Korn."

He tried a solo music venture that quickly fizzled. Then he became front man for a new band called Love & Death. He started a record label hoping to sign on Christian rock bands but struggled to attract artists.

"I'm going to get the word out there," he says. "Finally, after all that stuff in the past. I'm going to get Christian bands signed."

But the records didn't sell. He couldn't convince people to come to the concerts. The record label folded shortly after it started. And what was left of Brian's money vanished through bad investments and shady characters.

"I lost my Bimmer. I lost my house. Every business that I chose to get involved with crashed and burned within three or four years. I got to the point where I was looking for quarters in drawers to get my daughter lunch at school. My spirit was fighting to live in faith. It was like a baby when you take away the bottle."

Meanwhile Jennea was growing up to be a troubled teen. And despite Brian's best intentions, she just didn't have the emotional support and parental presence she needed. "Things would affect me," Jennea says, "like my mom being gone and my dad not being the most emotionally dependable."

Brian was often away from home as well, working on his new

ventures, and his absence took a toll on Jennea's life. But when he took her on the road with him, she suffered from being away from friends, routine, even a normal school.

"Things got worse for her," Brian says. "She would do her homework sometimes at three in the morning. People offered her drugs. It was like I couldn't win."

"Life was awful," Jennea remembers. "I didn't want to feel this way, but I did. I tried other things that I thought would feel better and help, but it made it worse. The truth was that I was hurting and I didn't know why. I wanted someone to help me."

Brian began to realize that following Jesus puts you on a path, not a destination. He didn't know how to do life or to function in healthy ways. He wanted to father Jennea well, but he didn't have the skills or know where to find them.

"Jennea began falling down a deeper hole from then on," he says. "Depression, suicidal thoughts, saying suggestive things that no father wants their teenage daughter to say online for other people to read. One day she got so mad that she told me she was cutting herself because of me."

Jennea needed help but didn't know what it looked like or how to ask for it. She hurt and didn't know why or what to do about it. She cried often and didn't know how to stop.

"I just wanted someone to realize I was hurting," she says. "I'm here. What do I do?"

Jennea's desperation climaxed in a suicide attempt. She'd heard you could kill yourself by drinking soap, so she tried it. It didn't work. But Brian got the message. He found her a counselor and sought out help. But the need for help also felt like failure.

He'd quit Korn to father Jennea, and now Jennea's life hung in the balance. It brought him to a cliff of doubt.

"I was like, 'Screw you, God. Who are you? Why didn't you let me die from drugs? Everything's going wrong. I try all this stuff. I follow you. I give to the poor. I gave up everything for you. Now my daughter's cutting herself. I have fits of rage. I'm stressed out. No one wants to come to the concerts."

Angry at God, he struggled to hold on to the faith for which he'd left everything. Years earlier he had stood up in a church and explained to the world that he'd quit Korn to follow Jesus. He wanted to be a better father. He wanted to follow the destiny God had for him. But that destiny had turned out to include a lot of disappointment.

Brian and Jennea desperately needed a new start. So Brian enrolled his daughter in Awakening Youth, a residential therapeutic boarding school. The faith-based school, founded by Tiffany and Travis Claywell, provides an environment where struggling youth can find a vision for their lives, build relationships, and restore their damaged relationships.

"Jennea needed a mother figure in her life," Brian says. "Tiffany is not her mother, but she's a female who's speaking nothing but strengthening stuff in her life. She's loving her with tough love and feminine love all at once. She needed it to make her a stronger person."

It wasn't easy for Brian to leave Jennea, the only thing he had left in the world that he truly cared about, at a school halfway across the country. "It was like a death," he remembers, "but it was also like a new life taking place. If you think of birth, it's messy and painful, but afterward you get to hold a miracle."

In the moment, a person doesn't often see when life pivots. It's in looking back that you see why everything happened as it did. That was true for Brian.

"There is a time that you have to walk away and let God cleanse your soul," he says. "It's like when you get a pumpkin and you scoop out all the guts and you put that candle, that light in there. God scooped all that crap out of me for eight years. He put that light inside of me. That's what needed to happen."

Slowly, over time, with a lot of help, life began to get better. Brian learned new skills; so did Jennea. They learned to talk and not yell. They learned to heal and to forgive. They learned to be a family.

"God allows things to come into your life, to feel like it's crushing you," he says, "because it squeezes out all of the impurities. That's how you get cleaned in your soul. I see that now. It's just like God saying, 'If you can just hang in there and watch what I can do, I'm going to restore all things.'"

New life also came to Brian's musical career. He still toured with his new band, Love & Death, and landed a gig at the Carolina Rebellion rock music festival. His old band, Korn, would headline the event. "I didn't let that stop me," Brian says, knowing the awkward encounter that could result with his former bandmates.

In his absence, Korn had released four studio albums, but the band never felt as complete or whole. And relationships between the band and their former guitarist remained mostly estranged.

The band felt hurt that he had abandoned them. He felt hurt by the lifestyle they had encouraged. Years had gone by since they talked. But now that they were in the same location, he decided to go and talk with them.

"We were just asking forgiveness for everything," he says. "We've known each other so long. It was real emotional."

The first sign of healing appeared when Korn invited Brian to play with them that evening. It wasn't a PR stunt or an attempt to get him back in the band. They just invited their old friend to come out and play. The surprise performance lit up the crowd.

"I could tell he just felt happy," Jennea says of her father.

He had joined the band so many years before just hoping to make money, party, and play music. But now his life had a new aim and a new clarity. Drugs didn't hold him captive. Money and fame had lost their appeal.

He thought of his fans. Korn's music expressed the pain and anger they felt in their lives. They connected with the music because it named the angst of their souls and the troubles they faced. But what if Brian could go back to his people and tell them the peace he'd found?

"It all seems to make sense," Jennea says. "God puts us through things so we can be prepared for the next thing. Dad has matured amazingly. He's managing his emotions, learning how to talk with me, and taking the time."

Meanwhile Jennea had graduated from Awakening Youth. She now attends university and serves as a communications assistant for Awakening Youth. She has a new strength in her and a clear vision for a greater life. "I have always wanted this in my life," she says. "Normal friends, normal home, normal times when I do things. I finally have it. I finally got what I asked for."

Looking back, she can see how far she has come. "Like any other young teenager, I struggled with low self-esteem and peer pressure. Those things really took their toll on me. I found myself at rock bottom. Words cannot express how grateful I am and how much growth I've gone through, how much transformation and healing. God has completely shown himself to me, and it's amazing."

Cleansed of his old life, Brian decided God's path led him back to Korn. "He put that light inside of me," he says. "That's what needed to happen. And now I'm going back by the leading of the Lord to my people to hang out with them."

Shortly after his surprise appearance at Carolina Rebellion, James "Munky" Shaffer, his old bandmate, called him about playing on a new album. "I don't want this to be about you coming back," Munky said. "I just want to see you as my old friend. And I love being reconnected with you. If you feel like you want to do this, the door's open. Let us know."

With that, Brian flew out to California to help write the next album.

"It was instantly a positive energy in the room," Brian says. "We went to eat at my parents' house, like old friends just breaking bread. I went on the road with them for another month. It got better and better and better."

In May 2013, Brian officially announced he rejoined the band.

"I left it once; I'll leave it again," he says to those who fear this new development endangers the progress he has made. But a new person has emerged in the eight years of his self-exile. You won't find Brian partying after his shows. You'll find him talking with his fans, telling them his story, even praying with them.

It's an extreme version of what Jesus once said in praying for his followers, "My prayer is not that you take them out of the world but that you protect them from the evil one. . . . As you sent me into the world, I have sent them into the world."[1]

God had to take Brian Welch out of the world for a time. He took away the drugs and the partying. This much Brian knew he needed to be rid of. But God had more to scoop out. He took away Brian's money, his self-importance, even his own daughter. When he had nothing left, God said, "You still have me."

God hadn't abandoned Brian in those years. God remade him. He had ended his old life to begin a new and better life. In Jesus' words, he'd been born again. But before he could be fully healed, he had to cut away all that clung to him. The surgery bled him and cut him deep, but the Surgeon knew his cuts would save Brian's life.

Some people think those who follow Jesus will have perfect, easy lives. Brian Welch learned that's a lie. For him, following Jesus meant entering a fire where God would burn away everything he treasured. Only as he came out of the fire did Brian realize the beauty of this divine plan. The greater life that God promised meant ending his old life. It really was a new birth, with all the pain and mess.

This truth isn't just for rock stars and drug addicts. It's for all of us. Whatever you face, you'll find that pain is God's most enlivening tonic. It cleanses and clarifies. It's not pointless, though despair will tempt you. It's not vindictive, though doubt will plague you. It's the work of a Doctor healing a patient he loves. He's creating life from death, beauty from ugliness.

Lauren Scruggs Kennedy learned this sharp and difficult lesson through a traumatic injury that nearly took her life. Her parents had shared their story through I Am Second shortly after we first filmed Brian Welch. We never imagined we'd have them back in the studio, this time to tell how they almost lost their daughter.

Chapter 12
Beauty

I was ugly and ruined

LAUREN SCRUGGS KENNEDY, LIFESTYLE BLOGGER

Cheryl Scruggs and her twenty-three-year-old daughter, Lauren, showed up for a holiday party at a friend's place. Their friends lived adjacent to a small airport and owned their own plane. The friends offered to take a group of partygoers up to see the Dallas cityscape lit up for the holidays. Lauren longed to see the view, so off she went, leaving her mother at the party.

Shortly thereafter, a young girl ran back to the party with horror written on her face. "Lauren's been hit by the airplane propeller," she said, eyes wide and full of tears.

"I just stood there," Cheryl says. "I didn't even know what to do. It wasn't registering with me what was going on."

Finally her mind caught up with the words, and she set off running toward the hanger.

"I could see her lying on the ground, face down," she says. "She wasn't moving. She was lying in a pool of blood. I didn't know if she was even alive."

Cheryl bent down to her daughter. Tears filled Cheryl's eyes and choked her voice. She put her lips to her daughter's ear.

"Mom's here," Cheryl said. Lauren made a noise. She was alive, but barely.

The propeller had severed Lauren's hand, broken her collarbone, and cut deeply into the left side of her face. The next minutes and hours would determine much of Lauren's future. They rushed Lauren to the hospital, where she underwent eight hours of surgery. She'd lost her left hand and eye and suffered severe head trauma. The doctors couldn't say if she'd ever speak again or if she'd even have the same personality.

"All I knew to do was just pray and keep calling out to God in that moment," Cheryl says. "I felt helpless. As a mom, you never dream that your child is going to go through anything like this. I couldn't give her hand back to her. I couldn't save her eye. I knew she would be affected by her hair being shaved on the left side of her head. There was nothing I could do to change it."

Lauren's brain showed early signs of recovery. She could speak again within a few days. Her personality reemerged. They thanked God for the miracles, but the emotional battle would now begin.

Traumatic injuries don't just hit the body; they also affect the mind and touch the soul. Could Lauren ever accept the altered face that would stare back in the mirror? Could she trust a God that allowed it to happen? Would she ever find the new path her life must now travel, or would she lose herself on the journey?

The Scruggs family had journeyed similarly dark paths before, not so physically dramatic, but equally challenging—especially Cheryl's divorce from her husband, Jeff, when Lauren was quite young. It's in those dark moments that the hardness of life crashes against the tender promises of God. How could a loving God let your marriage fall apart? Or allow an airplane blade to rip through your daughter's body?

"Jeff and I got married thinking we could complete each other," Cheryl says, "that we somehow could make each other whole. But I wasn't whole. I felt empty. I was missing something. I got it in my head that it was Jeff's fault that he wasn't meeting my needs."

One day, tears just burst down her face. She wailed in agony. Jeff ran in at the sound of her crying.

"What's wrong?" he asked, rushing to her side, putting his arms around her. But she pulled back, disgusted by his touch.

"I don't know if I love you," she said. "I don't know if I've ever loved you." She could hardly believe the words that came out of her own mouth. She'd never intended to say them, but she felt them.

Jeff, dumbfounded and confused, had no answer. He couldn't understand his wife's pain and loneliness. He couldn't, at the time, see his part in her pain. She would soon find solace in the arms of another and shortly afterward divorced Jeff.

"I got a divorce because I had thought Jeff would fill the hole that only Jesus could fill," Cheryl says now, looking back. But she learned too late that no human could fill such a hole. She had hoped to fill a God-size hole in her heart with a human-size relationship. When she finally did see the truth, the damage had been done.

"I looked behind me and I saw the wreckage I had left behind," she says. "I had made a huge mistake, but how could I undo all that?"

She wrote a letter to Jeff and read it aloud to him. In it, she owned all her mistakes and failures. She begged forgiveness and asked to try their marriage again. That letter started a long and winding journey for their whole family that eventually led to their remarriage after six years of divorce.

"Early in our first marriage," Jeff says, "our satisfaction came from all the things, all the worldly things, the possessions, the great house with the ocean view. Now we realize that stuff is junk. We learned that our marriage takes three—me, Cheryl, and Jesus. We learned that marriage only really works when Jesus is first."

They would have to bring this truth into their present crisis if their family was to make it. Lauren had survived, but that was about it. Her body was disfigured, and her emotional state was precarious. "Anger was my first response," Lauren remembers. "I thought I was ugly, that nobody would ever love me. I thought my life was ruined. The anger would come in phases. I would cry or yell, push my dad. I would be fine one day and angry the next. In some of my hardest days, I would just ask to see my twin sister, Brittany."

Brittany would come over from work and just sit with Lauren. A peace came with her presence. She didn't need to talk or explain.

Their mother would come in at night and sleep beside Lauren, praying as she did. Jeff would read from the Bible, especially from Psalms. The poetry spoke of doubt, pain, and yet still of faith.

"They reminded me that the Lord had sweet purpose in what had happened," Lauren says. "He wasn't punishing me for anything. He had purpose in it."

This understanding wasn't new to her, though it was being tested in much harder circumstances. Years earlier, she had learned that pain isn't a sign of chaos or divine indifference but of an orchestrated plan by God to bring healing to the lives of others.

"My faith formed when my parents were divorced," she says. "Brittany and I decided to pray that they would get back together. We would pray every day, just trusting the Lord was bigger than what we thought was possible. It really formed my trust in him and helped me see his grace and his purpose. Something that looked negative to us really touched a lot of people, changed a lot of marriages."

After they remarried, Jeff and Cheryl eventually started Hope Matters Marriage Ministries to help other couples who were struggling. Their book, *I Do Again*,[1] brought help to thousands of marriages. Their remarkable story of divorce and remarriage continues to inspire people around the world.

Lauren witnessed her parents' journey and learned from it that God had a plan for all their struggles as a family. No one would ever choose the pain of Jeff and Cheryl's story, but God had used it to bring relief and healing to so many others. Lauren believed she would find some purpose for her own pain as well.

"I never experienced anger toward the Lord," she says. "I knew that he was sovereign. I knew he knew what he was doing. I felt anger toward the situation. I wanted my hand back. I wanted my eye back and my old face back. I couldn't fix that, but the Lord is the one who was in control."

"My family was my rock during this whole thing," she says. "They daily reminded me of the Lord's unconditional love. They would always be by my side. And having them around me reminded me of how the Lord had put our family back together. It was celebrating that as well.

"Every day I see and understand more of the purpose that he has in what happened to me. From the messages I get from people and the people I meet in public who recognize me, I see a purpose in it. I think I'm seeing that this life is way bigger than me. I want to stop being so self-fulfilled and shut off the idols of appearance or attracting men or other things I've often looked to."

Before the accident, Lauren had been a rising fashion and lifestyle blogger. She'd interned with top fashion brands in New York City before venturing out on her own with a blog and online magazine.

"I found my voice in writing," she says. "After my experiences in the New York fashion scene, I decided to start a magazine and use my love for writing and business. I had a mentor in the fashion industry who had two online magazines. She trained me and really encouraged me to start my own magazine. She unleashed the vision I had for it and the inspiration to pursue that area of my life."

"But a lot has changed about my career aspirations," she

says. "I've gained a new perspective on life. Things have deepened for me. A lot of things that I held important earlier, even in my career, were quite shallow. I just want to use what I've been through to encourage other people. I want people to know that our appearance is not what defines us. Even insecurities that we may hold onto don't define us.

"God has called me to be open about what I've been through, to be vulnerable. Even though it's something that I would not have personally chosen for myself, it shows that God has such a different plan. It's shocking and unexpected, but it's still something really beautiful.

"I have a lot of peace now. Every day I have realized I need to walk by the minute. A lot of times insecurities will come up because I don't look how I used to. I fight them away with truth and Scripture. I experience peace daily, and it's amazing how God has put people in my life to help. Friends, my physical therapist, my church, my family—they have just wrapped around me, and they have been a huge influence on the peace that I have."

In 2012, less than a year after her accident, Lauren published her first book, *Still Lolo*.[2] She wrote her *New York Times* bestseller, *Your Beautiful Heart*,[3] in 2015. She has since married the love of her life, Jason Kennedy, and relaunched her blog,[4] where she shares her story and lifestyle tips aimed to inspire people to find balance and peace in life.

Lauren didn't choose what happened to her, but she did choose to find purpose in it. She chose to trust that God had a plan to use her pain to help others. Her choice to find purpose in the pain has given her a peace about her new life. She still has moments of doubt and struggle, but she doesn't live in those places. She lives in the current moment and in the hope of the future. She accepts the present and believes something greater will come in the future.

But not every story ends up with the hero married, happy, and a bestselling author. Sometimes it's just the opposite. Yet God still turns great tragedy into great good. How long it takes and what it looks like when it comes cannot be predicted. Sometimes, as with Austin Carlile, it looks like three suitcases and debilitating disease.

Chapter 13
Pain

the thief came

AUSTIN CARLILE, FORMER LEAD
VOCALIST FOR OF MICE & MEN

You've heard rags-to-riches stories before. A guy who is down on his luck gets a big break. He works his tail off. He has some challenges, a couple of close calls, but then he makes it. All his dreams come true. The camera pans out on a setting sun with the protagonist smiling and sipping sweet tea on his porch swing.

But what if you got to the sweet tea and the porch swing and hate the life you've found? What if the dream you spent your life chasing made you ever more unhappy the closer you got to it? What if this world couldn't give you the happiness and peace it promised?

This is the story of Austin Carlile, former lead vocalist of the rock band Of Mice & Men. At the time of his I Am Second interview he had nothing. He had no job, his health was poor, and all his belongings fit inside three suitcases. He'd fallen from the heady life of a touring rock star to barely making it. He sat down with us having nothing but his story. But as he puts it, "I have so much more joy, peace, and happiness now than I've had in my entire life."

The Bible frequently speaks of God refining his people with fire, purifying them like gold or silver in a furnace.[1] When the ore is harvested from the earth, it's mixed with rock, mud, and other impurities. The ancient art of separating the gold from these impurities involves melting the ore in a furnace. As the ore melts, the precious metal separates and sinks to the bottom while the impurities rise to the top. The artist then scrapes off the waste, leaving the purified gold or silver.

"That's how I see God," Austin says. "He gave me everything, and he took everything from me. And now the man that I've become—it's like I don't even recognize who I was. I don't know who that person was. He's made me into something new."

God burned away everything that wasn't gold in Austin's life, but Austin doesn't consider it a loss. God had a purpose in it all. You can't make gold without going through a fire.

Austin's fiery ordeal began with the divorce of his parents when he was fifteen years old. "It came out of left field," he says. "The home life was always good. There was always a lot of love. We didn't have many material things, but there was love. Having it ripped apart was a big deal for me. It was a shock."

One shock would follow another. After his parents divorced, Austin and his mother had moved out of state to restart their lives. Just as they were putting their new life in order, the phone rang. It was Austin's grandmother.

"My grandma told me they were taking my mother to the hospital," he says. "She'd passed out at the restaurant they were eating at. My grandma gave me the address for the hospital. I got there just as the ambulance arrived. They were pulling my mom out of the back."

Hospital staff escorted Austin and his grandmother to a waiting room. A short time passed. Then the doctors came in and told them his mom had passed. One moment he had a mother, and the next she was gone. They offered to let them see her body. But as they escorted Austin and his grandmother back toward her room, Austin darted for the exit.

"I ran out of the front of the hospital, threw my hands in the air, and I cursed God," he says. "For the first time in my seventeen years, I said words that I'd never said. This is where my life changed."

Austin immediately rebelled from all that he had believed in. His father had helped lead the worship music in various churches as he was growing up. Both his parents had taught him to believe in God and know right from wrong. But now, as Austin saw it, this same God had taken his family and his mother. That was not a God he wanted anything to do with.

"In the following weeks and months, I drank for the first time," he says. "I had sex for the first time. I did drugs. I got involved with a lot of violence, gang things. I was so angry at God for the divorce. I was so angry at God for taking my mom. How could he take her from me? I did everything in my power to rebel against him. Everything I knew was wrong I did just because I thought it would make God madder. I didn't want him to love me. I didn't want his love, because if this was his love, I didn't want any part of it."

Austin managed to graduate from high school shortly after his mother's death, but then he threw himself into his new lifestyle.

"I began running with people that I admired," he says. "They had shaved heads and face tattoos. They took me in because I didn't have a family. I didn't have anyone. I wanted to do anything that I could to kill the pain. That's also when music really came into my life. I saw it as a new god. I decided to put my time, my trust, everything I could into this, because it's something that I was good at.

"I started a band and we got a record deal. We started off in vans and trailers, playing for two hundred dollars a show. We'd beg people to buy our CDs and merch. I thought if I could just make the next step, the next tour, some more records, it would fill this hole in my heart."

Barely a year after starting the band, Austin had to take a break. After his mother died, an autopsy revealed that she had an aortic aneurysm that ruptured. The aorta is the body's largest artery connecting directly into the heart. The doctors linked the aneurysm on her aorta to a previously undiagnosed health condition—Marfan syndrome. This disorder affects the body's connective tissues, resulting in an array of potential health complications including heart failure, joint problems, and even spinal deformities. Since it is a genetic disorder, doctors tested Austin for it. He tested positive.

Knowing he had Marfan syndrome just fueled Austin's anger

issues. "I had all this rage. A lot of it was toward God. Music was the place where I could release all of that. I could yell into a mic and get all of that rage and hate out."

Through it all, Austin had to submit to frequent checkups, particularly for his aorta. When they found a bulge developing on his aorta—the same place that had ruptured and killed his mother—he required surgery to repair it.

"I wanted to do the surgery, be better, and move on," he says. "But I started having other issues with my hip, ribs, back, and legs. I started to get really bad arthritis. I started getting seizures in my legs. My health was always an issue."

But he pushed on. He got back on the road with his band as soon as he could. Doctors warned him that people with this condition needed to take it easy and not exert themselves.

"I wasn't even supposed to do sports," he says. "But I was jumping off balconies and jumping off of the stage, starting mosh pits. I was living a lifestyle that just wasn't good for someone that had as many issues as I did."

Drugs and alcohol also took an ever-increasing toll on Austin's health. He drank heavily and smoked marijuana. The pot usage started as a way to help the physical pain but grew into more.

"I smoked marijuana all the time," he says. "It helped with the pain physically, but I also used it to help the pain I was dealing with mentally, emotionally, and spiritually."

The chronic pain from Marfan syndrome eventually led to prescription drug abuse. "Doctors wanted to help, and a big way that they tried to help was by giving me medication," he says. "Real quick, I found myself taking pain medication every day, taking uppers and downers. I'd take things to help me sleep and things to help me wake up, a lot of stuff for pain. I began relying on these things."

Austin's band, Of Mice and Men, was a big success. They toured with all the big names in rock. The shows got bigger and bigger. Their albums climbed the charts. But nothing satisfied.

"I immersed myself in my music, my lifestyle, but it was always just another building block. I never appreciated where I was, always building for more. I'd do bigger tours, sell more records. I'd think things would get better. I was trying to fill this void. I didn't know what the void was, but I knew it involved my first love, which was God."

He couldn't yet admit it or even articulate it, but he knew his lifestyle couldn't fill the hole. The drugs and alcohol couldn't numb the pain in his soul. The music couldn't give him the peace he so longed for.

Finally, desperate for an answer to a question he couldn't quite put into words, he called his father.

The band had just played another show. There was a party in the bus. Austin climbed up to the roof just as the sun went down. He could hear the other bands still playing.

"I asked my dad what the purpose of all this was," he says. "What am I missing? What am I doing wrong? I'm depressed. I'm in pain. My band is building all this success and all of these things, but I still feel so empty and hurt and lost."

The conversation went on for a while, but one phrase that his father said haunted him.

"Where's God in your life?" he asked.

"The next couple of years with the band, that question was something that really stuck with me," Austin says. "I began reading my Bible. The question made me look for answers. I still had my lifestyle. I still had one foot in the world with the band and one foot in Christ. I was standing in the middle of the road. When you're standing in the middle of the road, you get hit by both sides."

Austin knew God wasn't anywhere in his life. He'd spent years running from God, cutting him out of everything he could. But the farther he ran, the deeper he had felt that inner anguish and emptiness. The answer to his pain was to turn around and run the other way. He knew that. But it would mean drastic changes—more changes than even he could foresee at the time.

"I started to become sober," he says. "I kept reading my Bible. My life started to change. We were recording an album, and I couldn't write anything other than what God was doing in my life and this change that I wanted and was craving so badly. A lot of that record I didn't even write. My heart was crying out to write about this journey, this budding relationship that I had started with God. I was coming back to my first love."

"God, I want to come back," he finally prayed. He set down his pen and just cried out. "I need you. I can't do this on my own anymore. I want you to use me. I give you my life. I give you my heart. Use it."

At the time he had no idea what that would look like, but he soon discovered it would mean leaving Of Mice & Men.

"I thought I was going to continue with the band and serve God along the way," he says. "But my health took a sharp decline."

That refining process that God uses with his people was working in Austin's life, and it was painful. Austin started having trouble walking. His back pain increased.

"Every time I would sing, I would have really sharp pain shoot up into my head and my whole body. I would convulse and have seizures. I would throw up because of the pain. But I kept playing and kept pushing through."

Finally the pain grew so bad that it forced him to stop. He needed surgery and rest. This wouldn't be a quick turnaround.

As it turned out, Austin had four tears in the dural sac, a kind of membrane that encloses the spine and contains the spinal fluid. Such tears are a common but debilitating consequence of Marfan syndrome.

"Every time I was singing," Austin explains, "I was tearing holes in that sac. The pain was due to the spinal fluid coming out. I ended up spending a whole month in the hospital and then healing and resting in Costa Rica. I talked with the band and told them that I had to leave. They knew about my new walk with God. Some of them had been at my baptism. And they knew that my health was a big thing. They carried on without me."

Austin decided to use his recuperation time for more than just physical healing. He knew he needed spiritual healing as well. He needed to see his journey with God through, to find out what God had planned for him. If God wouldn't let him stay in the band, what would he have him do?

"I spent my time in Costa Rica diving into my Bible and into prayer," he says. "I was cut off from the world, away from social media and even from a Wi-Fi connection. I felt God getting closer and closer. I started having this new joy, this new light, and new hope."

A year passed, and Austin experienced another dural sac tear. He could feel that searing pain run down his body again. He could barely walk, barely move. This would mean another surgery and a flight back to his doctor in the US. But now he didn't have the money for a plane ticket.

"When I left the band, I left all of it behind. Everything was in the band. I was in Costa Rica because it was cheap. I could afford to live there. Now I couldn't even afford to get back for the surgery.

"You have to take this from me," he prayed to God. "I can't do this anymore. I don't know why you're putting me through this."

The next morning was a Sunday. Austin headed to the church he had been attending. He still could feel the pain shooting down his spine. He got there and noticed a group of people near the back of the building that he hadn't seen before.

He introduced himself. They chatted for a minute. Then one young woman asked him a question.

"I feel God speaking to me," she said. "Are you having back issues right now?"

Austin could hardly believe it. He hadn't shown those people any signs of pain nor mentioned anything to them. How could they know? But when they asked if they could pray for him, he agreed.

"They prayed for healing," he says. "And as they were praying, God was telling them different pains that my body was having. I'm not usually a touchy, feely kind of a guy. Crying in public isn't a big thing for me. But I broke down."

The people in that group continued to pray with Austin for an hour. After they finished he bent down and touched his toes for the first time in two months. He felt so good that he went out and swam in the waves at the beach that day. He even played a little football.

"The pain was gone," he says. "I was healed. Even my neighbors noticed. They saw I wasn't limping. I was playing football. They asked if I had had the surgery, so I got to share my story with them. God was doing something."

Three weeks later God burned away what remained of Austin's old life. When he moved to Costa Rica, he had put everything he owned in a storage unit in California.

"It was filled with everything that I had ever owned," he says. "Everything that I had from childhood. It was a lot of fan mail, my first instruments, my comic-book collection. I had my vinyl collection there, my recording equipment. I even had my mother's ashes in that unit."

But Austin's automatic card payment stopped working while he was in Costa Rica. The owners of the storage unit didn't have a way to contact him, so they auctioned everything off.

When Austin learned what had happened he broke down. "I didn't understand," he said. "I wanted my mom's ashes, my family photos, the only letters that I had from my mom. And I couldn't get them back."

Grief and anger surfaced first. His friends told him to sue or blast the company on social media.

"But I didn't want to do any of that," he says. "I thought it was so wild that God had healed me and then taken all of this from me. I lost everything. I have three suitcases of stuff to my name. This was just three months ago, but ever since I lost that storage unit, I have had so much more joy and peace and happiness than I've had in my entire life. I saw that everything God's done, everything he's taken from me, he's done to me for a purpose. He was refining me like gold."

"I still don't have anything," he says. "I don't have a job. I don't know what's next. I don't know what God's planning. He showed me that everything I need is in him. That's why he's so important to me, because I don't have anything else. I literally have nothing else, but my heart is fuller than it's ever been in my entire life.

"Jesus said that the thief comes to steal, kill, and destroy, but I have come so that you may have life and life more abundant.[2] That resonates with me. It's just plain and simple. Jesus came to build your life, to build you, to give you life. Man, is it a joy to walk in it."

Difficulties have a way of clarifying the big picture. They make you sit down and assess whether all those little worries in life really matter. Few people ever stop to think deeply about life or God when all is going well. You don't look for water unless you're thirsty. You'd be strange indeed if you went around looking for hardship, but when it comes it can give you a unique opportunity to find clarity. Austin Carlile's story shows us that it's in the dry moments of life that you are closest to finding the water.

God uses our dry moments to show us the need for the water. He uses pain to convince us of the need for healing. Austin

Carlile could blame some of his struggles on his diagnosis. Lauren Scruggs could focus her frustration on a freak accident. But what if those dry moments in life didn't have an outside cause you could pin things to? What if you felt you were to blame for your troubles and failures?

It can be easier to face hard times when they are not your fault. Chance and circumstance relieve your sense of responsibility. They let you say, "Well, I did my best." But what if you didn't do your best and you knew it? This is where Lynsi Snyder, owner of In-N-Out Burger, found herself.

൪# Chapter 14
Expectations

in-n-out of failure

LYNSI SNYDER, OWNER OF IN-N-OUT BURGER

For more than seventy years, In-N-Out Burger has basi-cally had only three items on their menu: burgers, fries, and shakes. They own no freezers, no heat lamps, and no microwaves. They have no franchises. And they have been run by the same family since Harry and Esther Snyder opened up their first drive-through hamburger stand in Baldwin Park, Los Angeles, in 1948. This simple but wildly successful fast-food chain now has more than three hundred locations nationwide. The company is run by Harry and Esther's granddaughter, Lynsi, who was thrust into the family business at the age of seventeen after the untimely death of her father.

"I had an attorney as a teenager," she says. "I had to make my will. I had trustees and a lot more responsibilities. My life was different than my peers, but it didn't change the fact that I was just a person like anyone else. I struggled with all the same things."

Guy Snyder passed in the middle of the night from a prescription drug overdose. He had long fought his demons, and he finally lost the battle on the night that Lysni had intended to end her engagement with then-fiancé Jeremiah.

"We had a fight," she says. It was late at night. Distraught, she drove to her mother's house in Shingletown, California, the Northern California town where they had moved after her parents' divorce.

"We were too young," Lynsi remembers about her breakup. "I wanted to go to school, move to Southern California, and just see where our relationship went. He just cried. He wasn't having it. I felt trapped. I didn't want to get married. I didn't think it was right, but he made me feel like he needed me."

Lynsi went to her mother and cried in her arms. She couldn't bring herself to share the real cause of her tears, so she blamed them on her father. He had earlier been rushed to the hospital with a suspected overdose.

"I miss Dad," Lynsi said.

"He'll be okay soon," her mother replied.

"No, he won't," Lynsi said. "The only way he'll be okay is if he dies." Those words would come to haunt her.

"Dad's death certificate says he died within five minutes of me saying that," she says. "I knew he was trapped. My dad had overdosed a few times. I once watched him in a coma for three days. I'll never forget holding his hand. They told me he could hear me, so I held his hand and I told him that I forgave him for abandoning our family because of the drugs. A tear formed in his eye. I knew he couldn't forgive himself. It was hard to see him fail, because I knew how bad he wanted to be a good husband and father."

Lynsi's earliest memories were of her father in rehab. She knew he couldn't pull himself out from under the addiction. Just as she expected, his addiction proved a deadly struggle.

Even though she expected her dad's addiction to end in death, Lynsi was devastated when it happened. "My world shattered," she remembers. "Deep down I just wanted his love. The connection, the bond we had—every child should have such a strong bond with their parent. His absence created a void in my life."

The void had first appeared many years before, when Lynsi's parents separated. Her father moved out, and his addiction and struggles grew.

"That's when I really started longing for his attention," she says. "My dad was the greatest source of love up until that point."

But now Lynsi's father wasn't gone for only a week or a month; he was gone forever. The hole in her heart grew larger, and to fill it she made an ill-advised decision.

"There was no way I was going to be alone now. I latched onto my fiancé and decided I wasn't looking back. I had to have a man to fill that void. No one put me in touch with Jesus, told me who he could be in my life and how he could fill that void. It was much later that I realized that."

Lynsi married Jeremiah just months after her eighteenth birthday. But when troubles came, as they do in every relationship, loneliness crept in. It threw her heart into a search for anyone who'd fill it.

"I jumped right into the arms of someone else," she says.

"There was an overlap in that relationship, which meant I'd committed adultery."

Lynsi looked at her sisters, who were both married and happy. They had kids and a relationship with her mother that she envied.

"I felt like a black sheep," she says. "I was the failure, the outcast. I knew I'd never measure up to what my mom wanted. We didn't get along well, so it was like I didn't have either parent. I started smoking pot and drinking. I had wanted to stay away from these after watching my dad, but now I just embraced being the outcast."

Still, Lynsi knew the straight path, and even in rebellion she couldn't completely quiet her conscience. Then a meeting with a pastor friend and his wife jolted her back to what she knew to be right. They took her to breakfast and reminded her where her present path would lead her. Her father had already walked that path before her.

"I prayed and asked God to give me the strength to do what was right," she says. "I knew they were right. And I couldn't just go back home from that meeting and go sleep with my boyfriend. I decided right then to make big changes."

For some people, the tale of their walk with God has just two chapters. There's the chapter before God and the chapter after God. God changes everything in their life, a light switch turns on, and their world starts spinning in the other direction. But most of us have journeys with detours and exit ramps long before we reach the happier conclusion. Lynsi was about to embark on a brighter part of her path, but darkness still lay ahead.

Lynsi wanted so badly to lay down those things in her life

that were not good, but she really struggled with doing it. "I could let go of the pot and the alcohol, but letting go of the guy was something different. I understood that Jesus could fill that void, but I hadn't felt it yet. I hadn't experienced it. I couldn't yet fully trust him with that."

Then that problem seemed to solve itself—or so Lynsi thought. Her boyfriend found God, too, and followed Lynsi in changing his life. The two of them agreed to marry just months later.

"It was the fast track," she says. "I told him that if he wasn't going to be a good influence in my life, I was going to let go of him. But then he changed. I felt it was okay if we got married. With that fear of being alone, I just went for it."

But both Lynsi and her new husband carried issues into the relationship, and soon they emerged. Ironically, part of their problems involved their new church. Time spent there began crowding out time with each other, and the marriage suffered.

"I couldn't understand it," Lynsi says. "I just wanted to be loved and appreciated and be worth his time. I felt that loneliness again, that loss of love. I didn't get the quality time I needed from him. And again I was tempted to receive it from someone else willing to give it to me."

Lynsi's loneliness led to another affair with another man. She'd promised herself never to make the mistake again, but there she was. The fact that she and her husband both taught and led at their church and now had two children (fraternal twins) made the shame of it even greater.

"I'd spent six years working for God," she says, "then I felt like I got handed over to the enemy and destroyed. My family looked at me in a different way. I couldn't recover who I was to anyone. I got hate mail from people I loved in the church. I couldn't get things right again. I'd screwed this up. How was God going to give me what I needed when I had messed up so bad? I knew he forgave me but didn't understand how deep his grace could go."

After her second divorce, Lynsi married the man she'd had the affair with. She married him to avoid that chronic loneliness inside of her. Deep down she knew that this relationship, too, would fail to bring her across that chasm of loneliness, but what could she do? She settled for what would at least dull the pain for a while.

Lynsi and her new husband were both involved in drag racing, a passion she had shared with her father. They also both brought in children from previous relationships. And both came seeking in the other what they could never find, but they knew nowhere else to look. Unfortunately, it wasn't long before husband number three began looking elsewhere.

"He cheated on me off and on for three and a half years," she says. "I felt like I deserved it, like I was paying for my past. It was the worst time of my life. Nobody ever talked to me the way that he did. He treated me like trash. I started to believe the lies that I deserved it, that God was punishing me. But I could not get divorced a third time."

Since the age of twelve, Lynsi had sought to fill the void in her life with men, but three marriages later she had nothing to show for it. The void in her heart remained and even grew. She felt lonelier, more miserable, more unloved than ever. The futility of her chosen path cried out to her. She could no longer soothe herself into believing a man could heal what was broken inside her.

"I was never willing to just let go," she says. "But now I was being pushed away, cussed at, yelled at, and cheated on. It was during that time that God took me to a place I'd never been before. When I felt more alone, more a piece of trash, more of a failure than ever, he was there. He was ready to love me and fill that void inside me. He'd been there all along. He just needed me to let go of that next guy. There was an awakening inside of me, knowing that God could call me out from all of my mistakes. Some people don't recover from those mistakes. It's amazing that he would use little old me, who screwed up so much stuff, to do great things for him."

It was at these darkest segments of her path that Lynsi saw God shine the brightest. Married but alone, together with someone who was really with someone else—it was in that loneliest of places that she found the love she had always longed for.

"I was alone," she says, "but I had Jesus. I had the Jesus that walked on water, raised the dead, healed the sick, and cast out demons. I had that Jesus. I had the real one, the only one filling the void, touching my heart. He saw me for who I'm called to be, not who I believed I was because of the things I had done. I still look back at those days of being alone and experience joy. I felt so strong with him, knowing that now I could be alone and be okay."

Realizing her husband had no intention of staying faithful, Lynsi felt God's freedom to end the marriage. She decided to let him go.

"Me and God were so close in that time," she remembers. "The loneliness, the emptiness was gone. That marriage really forced me either to be miserable and alone or to lean on God and find peace. When I came out of it, I wasn't perfect. I didn't always do or say the right thing. But my life totally changed. I knew that God had a purpose and a call on my life."

When things happen to you, you may wonder if God has enough love to care. But when it's you that has brought the mess, you're more likely to wonder if God has enough grace to forgive. You doubt if he's willing to put back the broken pieces. Lynsi wondered about that too—and the answer she found was life changing.

"All I wanted was to be used by God," she says. "I learned in those lonely times that though I was broken, he could fix me. The things I'd been through made me stronger. They didn't define me. God can still use me—that's what I heard from him in those times."

One year after filing for her third divorce, Lynsi began dating Sean Ellingson. And this time everything was different.

"Our relationship really is based on our love for God," she says. "Instead of being that fractured girl looking to fill a void, I am a whole person. He is a whole person. I've already done it my way, and that brought me a lot of pain."

Now Lynsi was determined to do things God's way. Sean and Lynsi married in June 2014. The reasons that brought her into this relationship are reflective of the healing she had found. She didn't come to this new marriage needing her husband to fix her or work miracles. She didn't need him to take away her loneliness and make her feel valuable. She entered this marriage already valued and loved, and being confident in that love gave her the freedom to truly love another person. And love made all the difference.

Some fall for the misconception that God only loves good people, whatever that means, or people whose lives are put together. The truth is just the opposite. Jesus even said, "I have not come to call the righteous, but sinners."[1] This may sound strange to ears used to hearing judgment. But God isn't sitting up in heaven looking for who he can judge; he's looking down for who he can forgive. He's looking for the messy lives that need him to clean them up. He's looking for the broken who need fixing.

Cody Garbrandt is just one such person. His life has always been messy, rough, and atypical, but he found a God big enough and strong enough to love him.

Chapter 15
Worry

tapping out of the fight

CODY GARBRANDT, MIXED-MARTIAL-ARTS CHAMPION

Cody "No Love" Garbrandt's job as a mixed martial artist is to fight to just shy of death. He is a former United Fighting Championship bantamweight champion and at the time of this writing the number-one-ranked UFC bantamweight contender. Yet his bloodiest fights never earned him a dime. When he was growing up, he and his older brother, Zach, tore up any apartment or home they ever lived in with their violent bouts.

"We fought so many times in our life," Cody says, "some pretty violent fights. Once we were at our adopted father's house. I brought over some friends for a night swim. We were loud. My brother had to get up early for work the next day. He's texting me to keep it down, keep it quiet. I ignored him."

Zach sent one last text and then came out of his room. He had a look on his face that Cody had seen many times before. He wasn't going to ask politely.

"Zach makes a face when he's about to throw some punches," he says. "He had that face then. I saw a knife next to me in the kitchen sink. I grabbed it and swung it as he came at me. I sliced his finger to the bone. He looked at me and punched the stove and shattered the whole ceramic stovetop. Then he wrapped his finger up with a paper towel and went back to bed."

The last fight they ever had started over a sandwich. Cody had left half of a Subway chicken sandwich in the fridge for later and Zach had eaten it. When a scuffle broke out over that, Cody and Zach were ordered to take it outside. So they did.

"There was a pump house where we would take people to fight," Cody says. "We would take them outside of the city limits where cops wouldn't go. It was a dirt road. People would pull off and park their cars. Zach and I went there to fight."

It was a duel of sorts, but not the gentleman's version. There were no refs, no crowds, just two brothers out for blood. The fight lasted nearly an hour.

"The reason I have this cauliflower ear was from Zach," Cody says. It's a mark typical of many wrestlers and professional fighters. When the soft outer ear suffers repeated blunt trauma, the skin can pull away from the cartilage and become severed from its blood flow. Bits of the cartilage die. The result is a swollen, pale, and misshapen outer ear.

"Zach punched me so hard in that fight that my ear just ballooned up," he says. "My knuckles were all cut up. My lip, my teeth were all busted up. It was one of those fights where I thought we might die, you know?"

That fight sobered both of the brothers up. They loved each other and didn't really want to kill or maim each other. They would never fight each other with that intensity again.

That doesn't mean either of them would stop fighting, though. Fighting ran in the family. In Cody's neighborhood, even the mention of their name evoked a sense of fear. "We were born into that tribe," Cody says. "People knew not to mess with the Garbrandt boys. They called us crazy."

Cody and Zach, born eleven months apart, fought from the womb. Cody, always the smaller and the younger, learned to fight back and never give up.

"He's the reason I'm so tough," he says. "My work ethic, that drive, comes from knowing there was always someone better than me. Zach was that person. You can see in pictures that we even fought as babies when he would steal my bottles."

Cody brings that fighting spirit into his current career as a mixed martial artist. MMA fighting is the brutalized ugly cousin of boxing. There's punching, kicking, grappling, with few rules. Two fighters go into a locked octagonal cage, and the winner is whoever comes back out. You win by knocking out, choking out, or otherwise forcing the submission of your opponent and, if none of that happens, then by a judge's decision.

"It's the most primal state we have as human beings, fighting another man for a better life," Cody says. "We all have stories and backgrounds that have led us into this octagon to fight each other. We each signed a contract. We each want to win the prize.

And the other guy—that's the man trying to steal a dream from me. He has the same thoughts that go through his head. He wants to knock me out, choke me, and steal everything from me that I've been working so hard for."

There's no giving up in the mind of a fighter. Cody walks into that octagon with *surrender* wiped from his vocabulary.

"*Surrender* is on the last page of the dictionary for a fighter," Cody says. "It's on your dying page, in the last chapter at the end of the book. That's the warrior's way. You go to battle with your shield, and you get carried out of the battle on it. There's no giving up."

As in boxing, competitors have coaches stationed outside the arena. The coaches have the task of ensuring the safety of their man. They have the power to end the fight if they fear for the life or limb of their fighter. But Cody rejects that safety net.

"I always tell my corner men that whatever happens in that octagon, I'm willing to die in there," he says. "If you guys got to carry me back out, then do it. Let me fight to the death. So *surrender* is a foreign word to me."

These encounters unleash something ancient buried in man's soul: the will to survive. If you win this fight, your family eats. If you win this fight, you have money you didn't have before. You have opportunities you didn't have. Either the other guy submits in pain or you will. It's these primal realities that compel people like Cody on.

Cody's identity as a warrior brings a grittiness to his version of faith. He doesn't live the meek, mild life one might expect of a good Jesus-following man. He purposefully gets himself locked into cages in order to destroy the faces and careers of other men who'd like to do the same to him. But there are truths that best preach in the heat of battle. There are things that warriors know that observers can only get by osmosis.

Sandpaper has a smooth side and a side that scours. So does God. He calls himself the Lord of armies and the Lord God Almighty. He's both the Prince of Peace and the Conqueror of hell. There is a ferocity about God, a warrior's spirit. Remembering this can be of great encouragement. When faced with the harder bits of life, are you confident that God is tough enough to scour them down?

"I didn't grow up in a church or go every Sunday with my family," Cody says. "But there were people in my life who preached to me and showed me the way to God. My uncle Bob was always there."

Born and raised in the little rust-belt town of Urichsville, Ohio, Cody grew up in an environment that prioritized toughness and hard work. His uncle took him to the local gym, where he learned to box. It was there that Cody got his nickname.

"It came from my uncle," he says. "He's the one that got me into boxing. He would take us to the gym, starting back when I was a teenager. My uncle was training a lot of amateur and local professionals. I'd get in there and spar with them. He would heckle them about me beating them up."

"This kid is here showing you no love," Bob would say. "You're getting beat up by a teenager."

The name "No Love" stuck. But Bob gave Cody more than just a nickname, and he taught Cody and Zach about more than just fighting. He told them that when he was young and serving time for various crimes, he'd had a strange encounter with the spiritual.

"He had an epiphany while in prison," Cody says. "I didn't even know what an epiphany was. But he would always tell us about his epiphany and the demons he battled with. One day, inside the prison cell, he felt like he was getting smothered. He couldn't breathe. He felt like the walls were caving in, his chest was caving in. Right then and there, he prayed to God to save him. He saw steam come out of him and hover in the corner."

From that moment on, Cody's uncle Bob gave up drugs and the crimes that had sent him to prison. He didn't know much about God, but he knew that God had saved him in that moment. When he got out, he told his tale to his nephews and to anyone else who'd listen.

"I looked up to him," Cody says. "I would listen to whatever he had to tell me. That was the first real sign of my journey with the Lord."

Uncle Bob often warned the boys about steering clear of mind-altering substances. "Nobody wins on drugs," he always reminded them.

"Our area is pretty stricken with a lot of hard, heavy drugs," Cody says. "He didn't want us to fall into that. My father was in prison my entire life. He was a drug addict. My other uncle was a heroin addict as well, in and out of prison—Uncle Bob, too, until he gave his life to the Lord. It really changed his life. God walked with him from there on out."

Cody's father and other relatives would sober up in prison

and then get out and go right back to making horrible decisions. But Uncle Bob gave all that up when he got out of prison. His experience changed him. He worked to pull Cody and his brother off the path so many in the family had followed.

"He was able to help us learn about God," Cody says. "He took us to church, took us to the message. He would pray for us before each fight. That's something that we still do today."

Faith can be passed along from one generation to another. When you are young you believe what you are taught. Questions and doubts may come later, but as a child you believe what those in your life teach you to believe. Eventually, however, there comes a time when you have to own your faith. You must choose either to hold onto it with your own two hands or walk away.

For Cody that moment came at a low point in his life, shortly after dropping out of college. "I tried to figure out what I was going to do. I felt like my road was running to an end. I felt unaccomplished. I didn't know what to do."

He had joined the wrestling squad as a youth and done well enough to earn a wrestling scholarship to college. Wrestling gave him a sense of purpose to school and to life. It kept him moving forward. But Cody quickly found out that higher education wasn't for him, and wrestling wasn't enough to keep him there, so he came home. He had to figure out the real world. He didn't have answers, and the doubts led to poor decisions.

"I got in with the wrong crowd. I started doing drugs and partying, living super carelessly. It almost consumed my life. My brother saved me."

Brotherly love is a strange animal. Punch a stranger and you go to jail. Knock your friend's teeth out and you've probably lost a friend. But brothers can fight one day and hug later that afternoon. Zach saw his little brother struggling to find his way and stepped in to help. He didn't have a lot of words, but brothers don't always need them.

"He came in, busted down the door, and gave me the biggest hug," Cody says. "He sat there and cried with me. That was the day my life changed."

The faith that Cody and Zach's uncle Bob had passed along to them became their own that day. They learned that whatever God had for their lives was better than the alternative.

"Those bad decisions led me to that," Cody says. "I wasn't myself. I wasn't happy. I was in a very dark place. It was at that point that we started going to church more."

Cody began fighting professionally shortly after this. He won six amateur MMA fights before signing with the UFC in 2014. He debuted against opponent Marcus Brimage, whom he defeated by technical knockout. He'd go on to win the next ten fights. In 2016 he fought against defending bantamweight champion Dominick Cruz and won, making Cody the new UFC bantamweight champion.

"There's a time and a place when you need to surrender to a higher power," he says. Surrender doesn't come to Cody's lips easily. He's made a living of not surrendering. But in his heart, he has found one place to bow his knee. In his profession, when you give up you lose everything. You lose the fight, the honor, and the prize money. If you had a title, you lose it. If you had a reputation, you give it up. That's because the men he fights want to take all that from him. But he learned to trust in the story his uncle told.

Uncle Bob had pleaded mercy only once in his life. In that prison cell so many years before, he learned that surrendering to God brought life, not death—a simple truth he taught his nephews.

"It's God's plan; his way that works," Cody says. "Once you give it up to God, everything's going to be okay."

It's a truth he learned from his uncle and tested in his own life. While he's not known for surrendering in a fight, he has found that life does require one point of submission.

Cody and his wife, Danny, had their first child just two months prior to giving his interview. "I'm new to fatherhood," he admits. "I remember being so nervous and scared of not knowing, almost like going into the cage. But it was a different kind of scared. I hoped for my baby to be healthy before he was born."

His worry and anxiety peaked as he sat one day in the parking lot outside of the gym.

"It was on my mind and my heart heavily," he says. "It was about two weeks before the arrival of my son. I remember speaking to God, 'Whatever you give us in this life, I'm going to give it to you. It's your work. It's your plan.'"

It was a cry of submission. When we have children, we tie up our hopes and our dreams in them. Some of us see in their faces a chance to right the wrongs of our own childhood and the failures of our adulthood. To lose a child is to lose that dream. It throws bitterness into all thoughts of the future.

Cody feared losing this dream, and worry haunted him as a

result. But he knew God's dream was better, and he surrendered himself to whatever God might bring in his life. Cody admits he's still young in the faith, still figuring out much in life, but he has this one point mastered.

"It's God's work," he says. "This is all God's plan. We're just a little part of his work. Once I surrendered, the last two weeks of pregnancy were a breeze. I knew it was going to be okay, whatever he gives us. I'm able to surrender to him."

God's plan isn't always what we expect. The path he puts us on is sometimes sweet and wonderful, sometimes dark and winding. What gives peace on that journey is knowing that it's the one God has for us. He knows every step and is bringing it to a beautiful end, even if the middle isn't so beautiful.

My wife and I prayed the same prayer as Cody did when we were expecting our second child, but we got a completely different answer than he did. We had to learn that peace doesn't depend on the journey but on the destination.

Chapter 16
Peace

when we lost Hope

DOUG BENDER, AUTHOR

I couldn't make the sonogram appointment.

The local coffee shop doubled as my office that day. The paperback version of my first book, *I Am Second*, hit the shelves the day before. I sat hugging a cup of coffee to work on final edits of my second book, *Live Second*. My editor had just emailed me that she needed to send it to the printer by Wednesday. I remember we had a couple of dead links to fix. I still wasn't quite sure where some of the commas belonged, and I needed to chase down a few more typos. In the back of my mind, I also stressed about the backlog of emails that needed answering from our launch team, which was helping to promote the book.

Today, we'd find out whether baby would need pink onesies or blue. But I'd told my wife, Catherine, that I wanted to make the appointment but didn't know how I could with everything landing that day. Writing wasn't even my main gig at the time. I still had another job that needed tending to. And other than finding out "he" or "she" we weren't expecting any big news. We'd had a miscarriage a year earlier, but the doctors had called it a fluke. They didn't expect any problems moving forward. None of us really felt nervous about today's appointment.

Catherine had decided to walk to the appointment with our three-year-old daughter, Bethany, who couldn't wait to meet our new baby. The idea that someone was growing inside of Mom blew her mind. It seemed impossible. I smiled as I thought about her excitement. Then the phone rang.

I screen my calls, especially on writing days. Exactly one person would get an immediate answer on a day like this. And when Catherine called, the phone didn't ring more than once. The news I got that afternoon made all the writing seem so much less important.

"The doctor said the baby is incompatible with life," Catherine said on the other side of the line. "She's giving her a 0 percent chance of survival."

That was the end of my workday. I sent off the book with a section still hiding some typos. I never did finish the rewrites. You can still find a few wandering commas in there. I drove to meet Catherine and Bethany and found them halfway home on the sidewalk. We cried. Catherine made some phone calls. We started grieving the loss of our healthy pregnancy.

"My friend Debi said something when I called her that has

echoed in my mind ever since," Catherine remembers about that terrible time. "She told me to not grieve what I hadn't yet lost."

The baby hadn't died yet. She was alive and still moving inside of Catherine. The doctor thought she would pass away within the month and certainly wouldn't make it two months. We were at week twenty already. They gave us the medical options. None were pleasant. We could end things early or let nature take its course. We decided to wait things out.

"I was lying on the couch feeling sorry for myself and upset with God," Catherine says. "I began to weep. I was mad that God wouldn't heal my baby. I held my belly and cried out to God. What I said I really don't remember, but I felt the baby move in me. It's like she decided to stretch out sideways and push on both sides of my stomach to give herself more room, saying, 'I'm still here!' I told her I was so, so sorry, and we went to sleep."

Our baby passed several weeks later. I didn't know this before, but when a baby passes in utero you still have to give birth. It's called a stillborn birth. As I write this, it's three days shy of the anniversary of that date. We commemorate it each year by releasing a balloon in honor of our little one and saying a prayer. This year we are planting a weeping willow tree.

Catherine processed the experience quicker than I did. She could cry and talk to people, which meant she had an immediate support group. She spent that first week on the phone with everyone and anyone. I, in contrast, hid in a corner. I went three weeks without even answering email from work and nearly got myself fired. I couldn't muster the words to explain why I went dark on them.

I couldn't talk. Talking about it made the loss of our baby more real, while keeping silent made it feel further away, like it had happened to someone else. My prayers dried up. What do you say to God in those moments? He's in charge of the universe. Doesn't that make what happened his fault?

They called what our baby had Trisomy 18, a chromosome-related syndrome that results in a 50 percent prenatal death rate. In my mind, that put things squarely in God's court. It wasn't something we did or something caused by environmental factors. Genes and chromosomes were God's domain, and so it was his domain that took our child.

All this hit at a time when the bulk of my professional life involved sharing hope with people. I was director of content for I Am Second, charged with overseeing every piece of written content that came out of the movement. I wrote or oversaw the books, discussion guides, web content, social media, even marketing and fund-raising material. Our mission is to inspire hope in people who feel far from God. I found myself becoming my own target demographic.

I brought the family on a fund-raising work trip in February, three months after we lost the baby. We drove from Texas to tour the East Coast from New York to Florida. On one particularly long driving stretch, Catherine and Bethany both fell asleep. I couldn't find anything but country music and static on the radio, so I switched it off.

"I don't know why you'd do this," I told God. I trusted him—that never was on the line. I just didn't understand. I knew he is a God of love, and losing a little baby to this terrible syndrome just didn't make sense in that context. How did death and love work together? Then I remembered asking him this exact thing years before.

My family had moved from upstate New York to south-central Virginia after my twelfth birthday. We'd visited a few churches, but I didn't really like any of them, although one had doughnuts, and I liked that. But then we visited a church just down the street. It was one of those really old, built-at-the-founding-of-the-town-type churches. It had an organ and gold-enameled, high-back chairs for the pastors to sit in up front.

Before the main service, the youth group met downstairs. I walked in, terrified of the room of unknown faces. I had left every friend I ever had in moving to Virginia, and loneliness had hit me quick and hard. Being homeschooled didn't help because I hadn't met many people my age yet.

One of the kids got up and helped lead the group in a few worship songs. He played drums. He had a cool-kid look about him. Cool kids had bullied me at my previous school, so I didn't have warm feelings for someone who had that look. But this guy changed my mind.

"Hi. My name is Daniel," he said to me. He asked me my name and introduced me around. He smiled and asked what brought me there that morning. He sat next to me. I could tell his friends sat in a different section, but he left them for the morning to keep me company.

I discovered that Daniel lived just three streets over from me. So I made a plan. He'd told me he rode the bus to school, which got out around three o'clock. I figured his bus would drop him off shortly after that. I didn't know his exact address, but I thought I could find him.

I put on my skates and wandered around his neighborhood hoping to "accidentally" stumble into him getting off the bus. My social anxieties were running really high at the time. I was a shy, lonely, socially awkward homeschooled kid who didn't have the courage just to ask Daniel to hang out when I saw him at church. I had to concoct this plan to get him to ask me.

I skated up and down street after street. I combed through the whole neighborhood, but I didn't see any school bus. Maybe I had missed it. Maybe it had turned onto one street as I pulled onto another.

I came back three days in a row hoping to find out where Daniel lived. On the third day I gave up. I had gone through every street in the neighborhood and seen no school buses. I decided I needed a new plan, so I began skating home. I turned down one last street on the way out of the neighborhood, and then I saw him.

My heart jumped. I nearly tripped, forgetting for a moment that my feet were strapped to wheels. I pulled myself together and nonchalantly meandered over toward the kids walking home from the bus stop. I spotted Daniel among them and said hi. My plan worked flawlessly after that. He invited me over, and I stayed through dinner. For years to come, this would be my second home. Sometimes it seemed I was over there more than I was at my own house.

Over the following years, my friendship with Daniel ebbed and flowed. I went off to college, and we didn't see each other much after that. We talked on the phone, and I always visited when

I came back to town. I didn't come home all that often, though, because I spent my summers interning at a place in Florida.

Daniel called me the day before I was due to drive back home from Florida one year. I missed the call. He turned up missing the next day.

It turned out that his call to me was the last one he made before he took his own life.

Daniel had been in and out of drug rehabilitation programs over the previous couple of years, but he had been sober for some months. He didn't leave a note or tell us why he had decided to kill himself, but our best guess is he was tired of hurting the people in his life. He just couldn't tell us again that he had relapsed, and he became convinced that it would be better if he left us. He was wrong, but we couldn't stop him. I came home to his funeral.

"Why?" I asked God. "I don't know why you'd do this."

Now, years later, I was asking the exact same question while driving along the highway with Catherine and Bethany asleep in the back.

"Why did you let this happen? Why did our baby have to die?"

I had no peace. And then I heard God's reply.

"I am still in charge," he told me. "Trust me."

The sky didn't split open with a booming voice from the heavens. I just had this overwhelming inner voice that could only be him. I wanted God to stop the pain and remove the wrongs of the world. People shouldn't die like this. I should not have lost my friend, and I should not have lost my baby. And God didn't give me the answer I wanted from him. He gave me the answer I needed to hear—the promise that he could still be trusted to fix what was broken in our lives. I just had to wait.

We called our baby Hope. Choosing the name was an expression of both our turmoil and our faith. We hated the loss and cried for God to give her back. The name *Hope* was a way for us to say that we trusted he would do so. We just had to wait. God didn't erase our problems or our pain, but trusting him gave us a peace while we waited.

I don't know what you are waiting on God for, but I can tell you he's worth the wait. He keeps his promises. I Am Second has spent the last decade telling the stories of people who have found him trustworthy. Some saw their prayers answered and their dreams filled. Some are still waiting. But all of them sampled enough of God's habit of keeping promises to know he'll pull through in the end. They each came out saying, "I am second. He is first. He will fix this mess and bring me peace."

This book is just a sampling of the stories we have collected. Our website hosts dozens and dozens more. We share them to inspire your own journey with God. The people in these stories come from every kind of background. They discovered God in love and loss, purpose and identity, difficulty and disappointment. They found him while searching anywhere and everywhere for answers. And at the end of their search, they learned that nothing in life compares to the peace of finding him.

The Bible tells this same story over and over again. God loves his people. His people run away and pursue their own desires. Apart from God, they find there is only pain, disappointment, and ultimately death. But God never gives up on his people. (He won't give up on you.) He sent his one and only Son, Jesus, to build the bridge back to him. Jesus died a gruesome death on a cross, was buried, and rose again three days later. In his resurrection, he accomplished the defeat of death itself, the ultimate enemy of us all.

Whatever your struggle, whatever your pain, God has it beat. He has a plan. I have told him often how I wish he would tell me more of his plan. I would like more of an explanation for some of the hardship I've faced. I'm sure you would too. But I can say, and I'll say it with the chorus of Seconds who have also shared their stories: he can still be trusted.

We have seen him.

We have touched him.

We have heard his voice.

We have found his peace while we wait for the day.

Trust Jesus.

Choose peace.

Acknowledgments

A special thanks to Keith Forster. Your story inspired me to build something greater with my life. The world is poorer without you.

Thanks to Catherine for your endless support and love. Bethany, Sam, and Isabella, I love you. Thanks to Ryan Jasper. You got me into ministry, and I'll always love you for it. Thanks to Mike Jorgensen, mentor, friend, fellow laborer, writing coach, and the one who gave his intern a chance to shine. I don't know what you saw in me, but I hope I can do the same for someone else. Thanks to Curt and Beth McClellan, our Texas family. You were there when we didn't have any other. Thanks to my parents, Gary and Michelle, for raising me in the faith.

Thanks to our long list of supporters and ministry partners. The list is too long to name all of you, but this book is as much yours as it is mine. Thanks for helping get the word out. A special thanks to the launch team—couldn't do this without you. A big thanks to the I Am Second team, past and present. It's been one

ACKNOWLEDGMENTS

of my greatest joys working with you to inspire hope. An extra big thanks to Nancy Nelson for her wonderful copy-editing eye. You are amazing.

Thanks to Casey and Eric Clark at Perked Up for all the endless cups of coffee. You kept me fueled. And to their team: Haden and Haley C., Ali D., Bayley C., Brittany K., Brooke H., Carly B., Charmaine S., Daniele I., Hannah J., Kristy A., Lynn S., Maddie, Paige B., Sarah J., Sarah S., Serena S., Seth J., Stefanie B., and Tara J.

All interior photographs © I Am Second. Credits as follows:

Kathie Lee Gifford: Fred Castelberry
Chip and Joanna Gaines: Stanley Tongai
Lee Yih: Stanley Tongai
Phil and Kay Robertson: Stanley Tongai
Ben King: Stanley Tongai
Shawn Johnson: Stanley Tongai
Eric Metaxas: Stanley Tongai
Albert Pujols: Stanley Tongai
R. A. Dickey: Stanley Tongai
Jason "Propaganda" Petty: Stanley Tongai
Brian "Head" Welch: Justyna Fijalski
Lauren Scruggs Kennedy: Stanley Tongai
Austin Carlile: Justyna Fijalska
Lynsi Snyder: Stanley Tongai
Cody Garbrandt: Justyna Fijalska
Doug Bender: Justyna Fijalska

Notes

INTRODUCTION
1. "Any Anxiety Disorder," National Institute of Mental Health (website), updated November 2017, https://www.nimh.nih.gov/health/statistics/any-anxiety-disorder.shtml.

CHAPTER 5
1. Philippians 3:20–21.

CHAPTER 8
1. Matthew 19:30.

CHAPTER 10
1. Psalm 139:13–14.

CHAPTER 11
1. John 17:15, 18.

CHAPTER 12
1. Cheryl and Jeff Scruggs, *I Do Again: How We Found a Second Chance at Our Marriage—and You Can Too* (Colorado Springs: WaterBrook, 2008).

NOTES

2. Lauren Scruggs with Marcus Brotherton, *Still Lolo: A Spinning Propeller, a Horrific Accident, and a Family's Journey of Hope* (Wheaton, IL: Tyndale House, 2012).
3. Lauren Scruggs with Lisa Velthouse, *Your Beautiful Heart: 31 Reflections on Love, Faith, Friendship, and Becoming a Girl Who Shines* (Wheaton, IL: Tyndale House, 2015).
4. Lauren's blog can be accessed at laurenscruggskennedy.com.

CHAPTER 13
1. See for instance Proverbs 17:3, Malachi 3:2–4, and 1 Peter 1:6–7.
2. See John 10:10.

CHAPTER 14
1. Luke 5:32.

About the Author

Doug Bender is a writer and small-groups coach for the I Am Second movement and organization. He developed many of the tools found at iamsecond.com and has coached churches, organizations, and individuals to use I Am Second groups to share the message of Jesus with their friends and family. He also works with I Am Second's parent organization, e3 Partners Ministry, as a church planter and pastor in countries such as Ethiopia, Colombia, and the United States. Doug and his wife, Catherine, have four children: Bethany, Samuel, Isabella, and Jesse.

Read more at iamsecond.com/book

I Am Second:
Real Stories. Changing Lives

Read the original national best seller.

Countless stories. One incredible ending.

A major league baseball player. A Tennessee pastor. A reality TV star. A single mom. A multi-platinum rocker. What do these people have in common? They've all hit bottom. And none of them stayed there.

Shocking in their honesty, inspiring in their courage, these stories are critical reminders that no one is too far from God to find him. Join these and thousands more who have discovered the life-changing power in putting God first and proclaiming, "I Am Second."

Live Second
365 Ways to Make Jesus First

If these incredible stories of changed lives have inspired or challenged you to reevaluate your relationship with God, then pick up this daily reader with 365 readings, prayers, actions steps, and an online community of support designed as a tool for you to Live Second.

"

If you're at a crossroads, or if you just need some clarity on where your life is headed and how to get there, consider taking this book for a spin. You'll be glad you did.

"

-Josh Turner, double-platinum country music singer/songwriter

Get more at **iamsecond.com**

Watch the Films

Watch the original, raw, and inspiring stories of real people telling how Jesus became first in their lives at **iamsecond.com**.

Follow and Connect

Get daily updates, inspiration, great stories, and more when you follow I Am Second on Instagram, Facebook, Twitter, or YouTube.

Join I Am Second for More Content

Get free exclusive access to all 140+ I Am Second films, plus behind the scenes content, practical tools, free downloads, and a Live Second Coach.

Buy Merch

Wear the gear that is sure to start a conversation. Get apparel, wristbands, and more. Everything you need to make your statement is at **iamsecond.com**.

I AM SECOND